STAR WARS

THE PHANTOM MENACE

THE EXPANDED VISUAL DICTIONARY

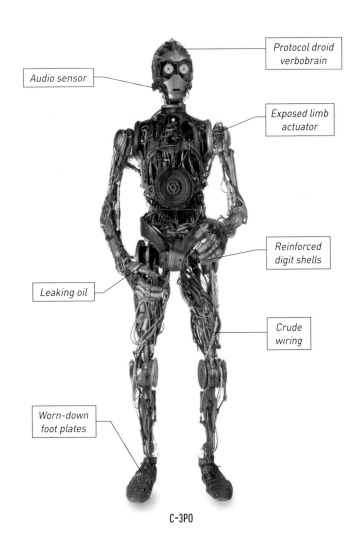

Audio sensor

Protocol droid verbobrain

Exposed limb actuator

Reinforced digit shells

Leaking oil

Crude wiring

Worn-down foot plates

C-3PO

Field generator
confines bird

Optional data-feed package

Full read
out display

PODRACE FAN'S
MACROBINOCULARS

Name of Theed
hangar engineer
Simon Jabesq in
Naboo Futhork

NEIMOIDIAN BIRD CAGE

Sound-damping
layers

NABOO HANGAR CHIEF
ENGINEER'S HELMET

Manual
start knob

Simple
ionizer array

Complex
ionizer
array

Heat radiator
shroud

TATOOINE GUNMAN'S BLASTER

Charge
generator
assembly

Sweeper screen stabilizes local
fields for delicate maintenance

Sand-tight construction

Cooling
unit

Hand-stitched
embroidery

Display confirms
transmission of
door entry code

WATTO'S IONIZER

Sunshield
fabric

Spinner motor

MOS ESPA COOLTH BACKPACK

GYRDA
KEYPAD

Sheer velvet
fabric with
tassel trim

JEDI LIGHTSABER

Carved wood from
forests of Naboo

HANDMAIDEN'S CHAIR FROM
THEED PALACE THRONE ROOM

Cycling field generators

Single antenna

COMLINK

STAR WARS®

BLISSL TUNER
(MUSICAL INSTRUMENT)

THE PHANTOM MENACE
THE EXPANDED VISUAL DICTIONARY

Written by
DAVID WEST REYNOLDS AND JASON FRY

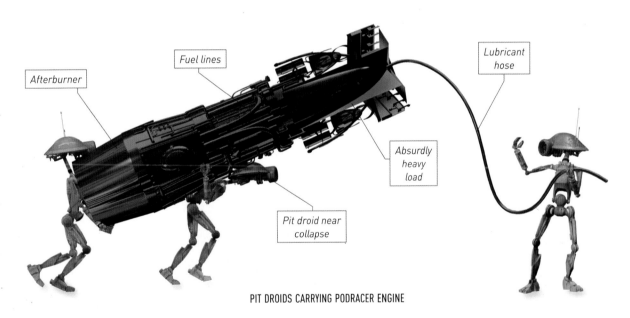

Afterburner

Fuel lines

Lubricant hose

Absurdly heavy load

Pit droid near collapse

PIT DROIDS CARRYING PODRACER ENGINE

Emitter assembly

LUCAS
BOOKS

DK

LONDON, NEW YORK, MUNICH,
MELBOURNE, AND DELHI

STATUE FROM SENATOR
PALPATINE'S QUARTERS

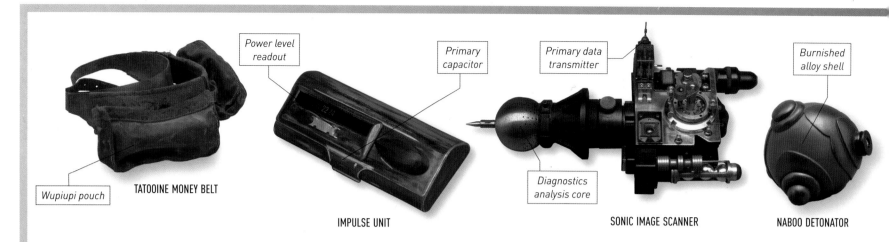

Power level readout

Primary capacitor

Primary data transmitter

Burnished alloy shell

Wupiupi pouch

TATOOINE MONEY BELT

Diagnostics analysis core

IMPULSE UNIT

SONIC IMAGE SCANNER

NABOO DETONATOR

CONTENTS

THE PHANTOM MENACE	8	BATTLE DROIDS	32
CORUSCANT	10	DROIDEKAS	36
MACE WINDU	12	QUEEN AMIDALA	40
YODA	13	THE QUEEN'S HANDMAIDENS	42
THE JEDI HIGH COUNCIL	14	PADMÉ NABERRIE	44
QUI-GON JINN	18	THE NABOO	46
OBI-WAN KENOBI	22	CAPTAIN PANAKA	48
THE NEIMOIDIANS	26	SPACE FIGHTER CORPS	50
THE FLAGSHIP CREW	28	THEED HANGAR	52
THE INVASION FORCE	30	R2-D2	54

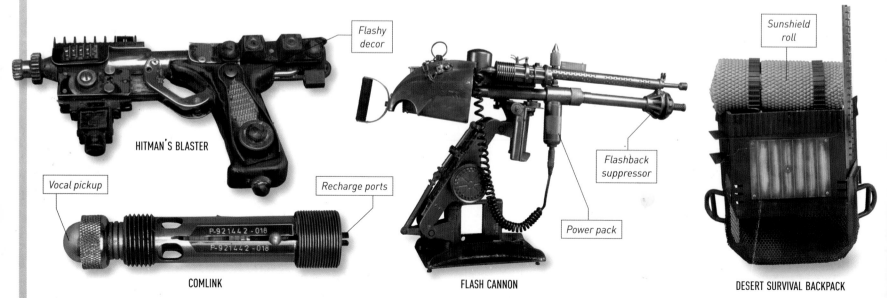

Flashy decor

HITMAN'S BLASTER

Vocal pickup

Recharge ports

Flashback suppressor

Sunshield roll

COMLINK

Power pack

FLASH CANNON

DESERT SURVIVAL BACKPACK

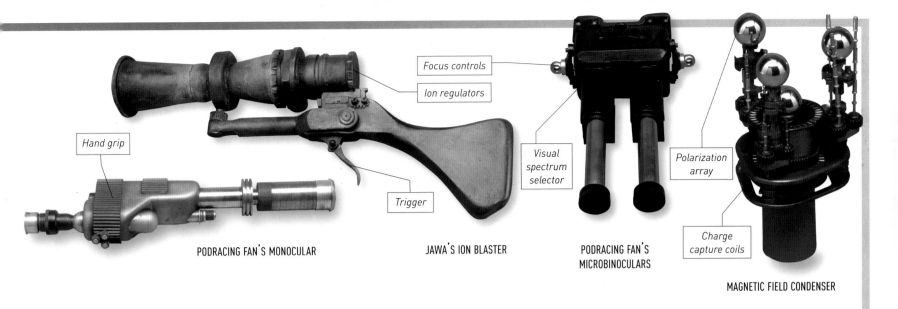

Hand grip

Focus controls

Ion regulators

Trigger

PODRACING FAN'S MONOCULAR

Visual spectrum selector

JAWA'S ION BLASTER

Polarization array

PODRACING FAN'S MICROBINOCULARS

Charge capture coils

MAGNETIC FIELD CONDENSER

JAR JAR BINKS	56	SEBULBA	82
THE GUNGANS	58	PODRACER CONTENDERS	84
GUNGAN NABOO	60	PODRACE CREWS	88
GUNGAN WARFARE	62	PIT DROIDS	90
SEA MONSTERS OF NABOO	66	THE PODRACE CROWD	92
DARTH MAUL	70	JABBA'S BOX	94
SHMI SKYWALKER	74	TATOOINE INHABITANTS	96
ANAKIN SKYWALKER	75	THE SENATE	100
FROM PILOT TO JEDI	76	CHANCELLOR VALORUM	102
C-3PO	78	SENATOR PALPATINE	103
WATTO	80	ACKNOWLEDGMENTS	104

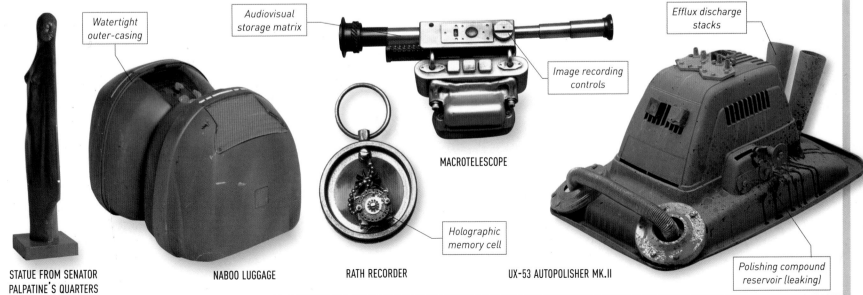

Watertight outer-casing

Audiovisual storage matrix

Efflux discharge stacks

Image recording controls

MACROTELESCOPE

Holographic memory cell

STATUE FROM SENATOR PALPATINE'S QUARTERS

NABOO LUGGAGE

RATH RECORDER

UX-53 AUTOPOLISHER MK.II

Polishing compound reservoir (leaking)

INTRODUCTION

IN 1999, THE LONG WAIT WAS OVER: THE *STAR WARS* SAGA RETURNED WITH
Episode I: *The Phantom Menace*, transporting audiences to an era often discussed but
never seen in the original trilogy. In this new era, Obi-Wan Kenobi is a young Jedi
apprentice and Anakin Skywalker just nine years old, his destiny lying before him.
The great, free Galactic Republic still stands, but is beginning to tear itself apart:
The institutions of government have become decadent and the galaxy's Jedi protectors
of peace and justice have dwindled in number. This is a time populated with fascinating
characters, whose worlds are replete with gleaming spacecraft, elaborate clothing,
sophisticated gadgets, and droids of all shapes and sizes. These artifacts tell a story.
They are clues to identity. From the deathly pale appearance of the Trade Federation
battle droids to the tasty gorgs of Mos Espa marketplace, *Star Wars: The Phantom
Menace—The Expanded Visual Dictionary* is your guide to the awe-inspiring worlds
explored in this exciting episode of the *Star Wars* space fantasy.

The original *Star Wars*: Episode I *The Visual Dictionary*, written by David West Reynolds
and published in 1999, offered a handbook to Episode I's new characters and worlds,
providing a wealth of information about what things were and how they worked.
Now, in this revised and expanded edition, it is time to travel back to the beginning
once again and immerse yourself in an enriched world. *Star Wars: The Phantom
Menace—The Expanded Visual Dictionary* considers the revelations of the following
two prequels, and draws upon the many new stories and extensive lore developed since
1999, including new art, stills, and cutaway views never seen before. Welcome back to
the galaxy far, far away, now richer and deeper than ever....

THE PHANTOM MENACE

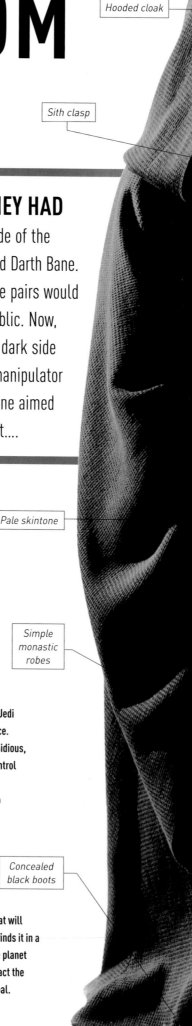

Hooded cloak

Hidden visage

Sith clasp

Pale skintone

Simple monastic robes

Concealed black boots

A THOUSAND YEARS AGO, THE JEDI THOUGHT THEY HAD finally destroyed the Sith: renegade Jedi who drew on the dark side of the Force for power. But the Sith survived in secret, reshaped by the Sith Lord Darth Bane. Only two Sith would exist at a time—a Master and an apprentice. These pairs would preserve the Sith teachings, waiting to strike at the Jedi and the Republic. Now, the Sith plot nears fruition. The Republic is weak and corrupt, and the dark side blinds the Jedi to their peril. The Sith Lord Darth Sidious is a master manipulator of Republic politics, while his apprentice Darth Maul is a deadly machine aimed at the Jedi. The Force is unbalanced and great change seems imminent....

Darth Sidious

The Sith Lord Darth Sidious sets into motion the final stages of his Order's 1,000-year-old plan to destroy the Jedi and usher in a new era of Sith rule. Working patiently, Sidious has extended his power and influence deep into the galactic government. Using his grasp of psychology and bureaucracy to stifle justice, he brings about the crisis he needs to make his move for domination.

SECRETS OF CORUSCANT
The city-world of Coruscant is the Republic's capital and home of the Jedi Order, guardians of peace and justice. It is also the hiding place of Darth Sidious, who works behind the scenes to control Senators, bureaucrats, and trade cartels—all pawns in his scheme to seize control of the galaxy.

THE SITH PLOT
Sidious seeks to arrange a crisis that will topple the Senate's leadership. He finds it in a trade dispute and an invasion of the planet Naboo—a phantom menace to distract the Jedi as the Sith pursue their true goal.

The Trade Federation

The shadowy figure of Darth Sidious controls the Neimoidian leadership of the cartel known as the Trade Federation. Sidious pushes them to protest Senate taxation of trade in the former Free Trade Zones of the outlying systems by blockading and invading Naboo, whose Senator Palpatine championed the new taxes.

Hangar arm

Detachable core ship

TRADE FEDERATION FREIGHTER

Sidious persuaded the Trade Federation to convert its commercial freighters into powerful battleships. The Neimoidians tell the Republic that they need this firepower to fight pirates, but they now control a mighty army—one that serves Sidious's schemes.

Antenna receives summons signal from Sith Lord

DARTH SIDIOUS'S SUMMONING CHIPS

Micro-screen

DISTANT SUMMONS

Darth Sidious uses a powerful hologram transmitter to communicate with his Neimoidian pawns. Specialized summoning chips signal when he wishes them to make contact with him. The Sith Lord rarely meets with his minions in person, preferring to remain a mysterious apparition.

Eye color altered by the dark side

Cloak of rough cloth

Multi-scan electrobinoculars

DATA FILE

▶ *Neimoidians assumed control* of the Trade Federation's directorate after six of its seven members were assassinated, leaving only Nute Gunray alive.

▶ *Gunray's deputy Hath Monchar* tried to sell the secret plan for the Naboo invasion to the highest bidder, but was slain by Darth Maul.

Maul has bided his time as Sidious's instrument, limited to secret missions against rebellious servants. He burns to reveal himself to the Jedi, simultaneously punishing the Sith's ancient foes and proving himself to his Master. He is delighted to be sent after Naboo's missing Queen and her Jedi protectors: At last the Sith will have their revenge.

Swords of the Sith

Fortified and twisted by the dark side, the ancient Sith fought constantly for power and domination. The hidden Sith are different: An apprentice serves his or her Master with absolute obedience, learning physical and mental discipline until powerful enough to one day claim the top spot and choose a new apprentice. Darth Maul is one of history's most dangerous and promising Sith.

CORUSCANT

A **WORLD ENVELOPED BY A SINGLE CITY, CORUSCANT** is home to the Republic Senate and, effectively, the center of the galaxy. Representatives from all member worlds congregate here to participate in the colossal enterprise of galactic government. As the most important Republic world, Coruscant is also home to great corporations; dreamers seeking to make their fortune in the galactic core; and an underworld made up of the poor, the desperate, and the criminals and plotters hiding in the shadows.

THE JEDI TEMPLE
The ziggurat and spires of the Jedi Temple rise a kilometer above a low-rise sector of the Coruscant skyline. The first Temple was built some 4,000 years ago around a mountain peak, and it has been enlarged and reconstructed over subsequent millennia. Home to the Jedi Order, the Temple is simultaneously a spiritual site strong with the Force, a repository of ancient lore, an academy for Jedi training, and a center of political power.

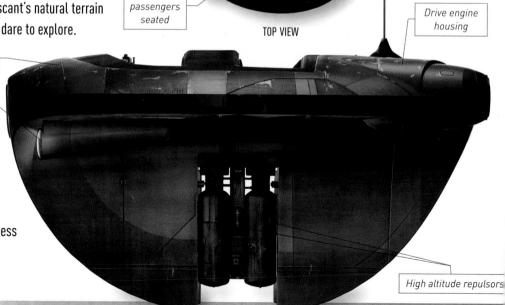

THE SENATE BUILDING
Located at the heart of Coruscant's austere government district, the Senate Building is surrounded by broad promenades lined with statues depicting the Republic's ancient Core Founders. The heart of the Senate Building is the Great Rotunda, where the galaxy's representatives and the Supreme Chancellor meet and debate.

Dizzying Heights

The tallest skyscrapers of Coruscant are 6,000 meters high, ringed with the constant flow of the planet's legendary airspeeder traffic. The entire planet is covered with layers of buildings, with new city blocks built right over ancient towers. Coruscant's natural terrain is lost beneath millennia of construction; below lightless levels few dare to explore.

Mild tractor field keeps passengers seated

Communications antenna

Drive engine housing

TOP VIEW

Guidance computer

Multi-spectrum headlights

Side-mounted repulsors cushion docking

Air Taxis

Air taxis carry passengers throughout the bewildering maze of canyons and pinnacles in Coruscant's skyscraper landscape. The planet's taxi jockeys are famous for their recklessness and gruff treatment of off-worlders.

Turbines offer rapid acceleration

REAR VIEW

High altitude repulsors

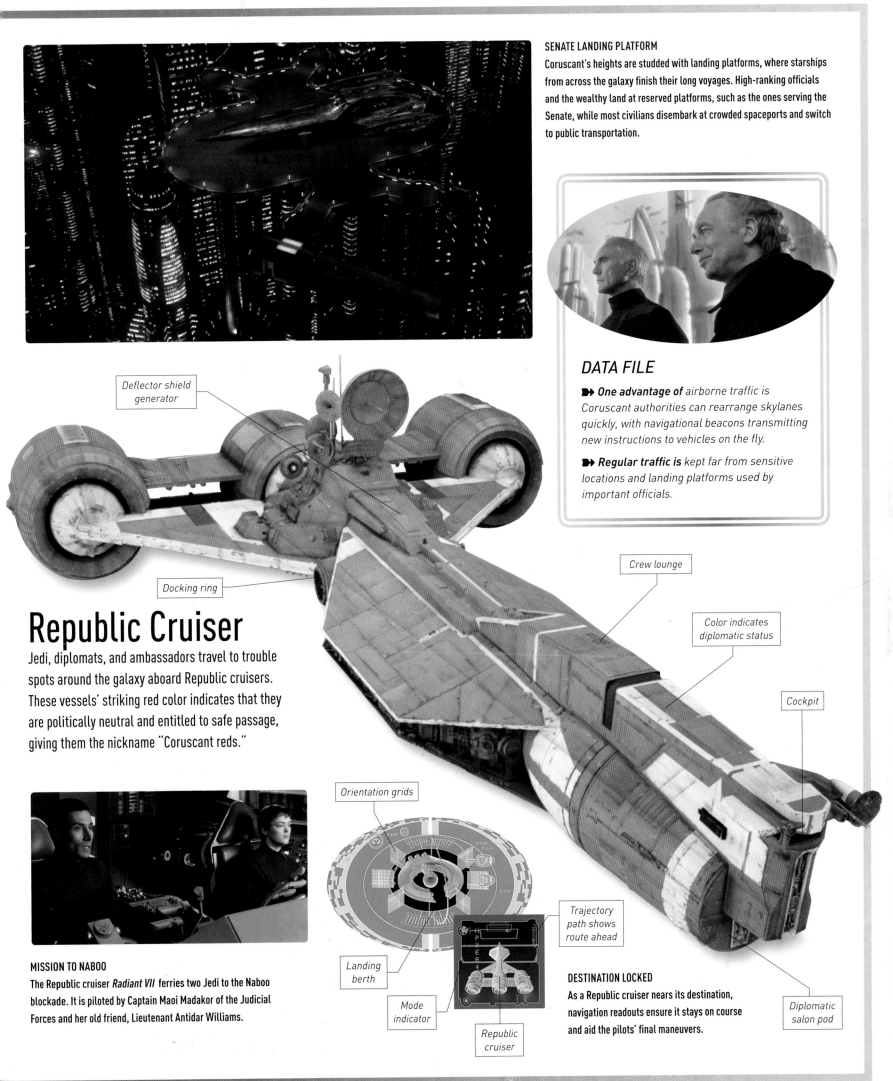

Coruscant's heights are studded with landing platforms, where starships from across the galaxy finish their long voyages. High-ranking officials and the wealthy land at reserved platforms, such as the ones serving the Senate, while most civilians disembark at crowded spaceports and switch to public transportation.

Deflector shield generator

DATA FILE

▶ **One advantage of** airborne traffic is Coruscant authorities can rearrange skylanes quickly, with navigational beacons transmitting new instructions to vehicles on the fly.

▶ **Regular traffic is** kept far from sensitive locations and landing platforms used by important officials.

Docking ring

Crew lounge

Republic Cruiser

Jedi, diplomats, and ambassadors travel to trouble spots around the galaxy aboard Republic cruisers. These vessels' striking red color indicates that they are politically neutral and entitled to safe passage, giving them the nickname "Coruscant reds."

Color indicates diplomatic status

Cockpit

Orientation grids

Trajectory path shows route ahead

Landing berth

MISSION TO NABOO
The Republic cruiser *Radiant VII* ferries two Jedi to the Naboo blockade. It is piloted by Captain Maoi Madakor of the Judicial Forces and her old friend, Lieutenant Antidar Williams.

Mode indicator

Republic cruiser

DESTINATION LOCKED
As a Republic cruiser nears its destination, navigation readouts ensure it stays on course and aid the pilots' final maneuvers.

Diplomatic salon pod

11

MACE WINDU

SENIOR MEMBER OF THE JEDI COUNCIL, MACE WINDU'S wisdom and self-sacrifice is legendary. In a long and adventurous career, he has repeatedly risked his life to resolve great conflicts in fairness to both sides. Windu is sober and cool-minded but is also capable of dramatic actions in the face of danger. Always ready to put himself at risk, Mace Windu is very reluctant to risk the lives of others. In particular, he is wary of fellow Jedi Qui-Gon Jinn's headstrong belief in Anakin Skywalker, and senses great danger in the boy. These concerns weigh heavily upon him as he considers them against his friendship and respect for Qui-Gon.

Under-tunic

Jedi robe

Tunic

Time and again, Mace Windu has stood at the center of great conflicts. His fame has only added to his negotiating skills.

Lightsaber

Mace Windu is one of the Jedi Order's best duelists. He alternates a blue-bladed weapon with a rare amethyst-bladed lightsaber. Mace and fellow Jedi Sora Bulq created the dangerous new style of lightsaber combat known as Vaapad.

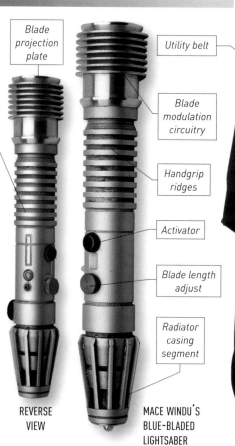

Blade projection plate

Cycling field generators

Utility belt

Blade modulation circuitry

Handgrip ridges

Activator

Blade length adjust

Radiator casing segment

REVERSE VIEW

MACE WINDU'S BLUE-BLADED LIGHTSABER

The Jedi High Council is secretly called upon by Supreme Chancellor Valorum of the Galactic Senate to settle the conflict with the Trade Federation. Mace Windu summons a pair of his most able Jedi for the mission. Windu little suspects the evil and danger awaiting Jedi Master Qui-Gon Jinn and his apprentice Obi-Wan Kenobi within the Trade Federation fleet.

DATA FILE

▶▶ **The Jedi use** the lightsaber as a symbol of their dedication to combat in defense, not attack, and of their philosophical concern for finely tuned mind and body skills.

▶▶ **Ambassadors, mediators,** and counselors, Jedi are warriors only as a last resort.

YODA

WELL INTO HIS 800S, YODA IS THE OLDEST member of the Jedi High Council, as well as its most deeply perceptive Master. A great traveler in his younger years, Yoda has visited hundreds of worlds on his own, spending years learning different lifeways and appreciating the infinitely variable nuances of the Force. Yoda takes a personal interest in the progress of Qui-Gon Jinn and his apprentice Obi-Wan Kenobi. Yoda recognizes their strength and potential even as he disagrees with some of their "dangerously reckless" choices.

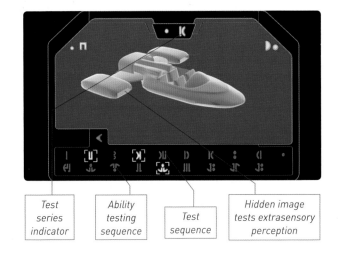

Test series indicator

Ability testing sequence

Test sequence

Hidden image tests extrasensory perception

Testing Screen

The Jedi High Council use multi-function viewscreens to test Jedi apprentices. These screens are built without buttons and are operated by Jedi mind powers. Only Force-attuned individuals can follow the high-speed series of images generated on screen. Testing screens keep the Jedi Council members in constant practice with their Force abilities.

Having seen so much of life, Yoda views all that happens with a long perspective. Less active now than in his younger years, Yoda remains one of the two most important voices of wisdom on the Jedi High Council along with Mace Windu.

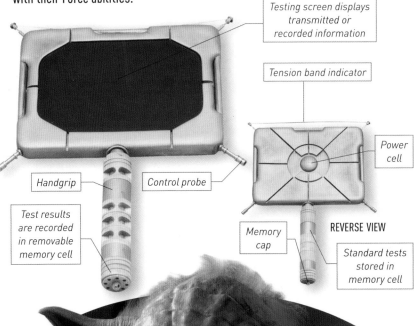

Testing screen displays transmitted or recorded information

Tension band indicator

Handgrip

Control probe

Power cell

Test results are recorded in removable memory cell

Memory cap

REVERSE VIEW

Standard tests stored in memory cell

YODA'S LIGHTSABER

Activator matrix

Blade emitter shroud

DATA FILE

➡ **Yoda's gimer stick** cane helps him to walk long distances and contains natural plant substances that aid meditation when chewed.

➡ **It has been** many years since Yoda has needed to wield his special lightsaber. Yoda takes quiet satisfaction in finding non-violent solutions.

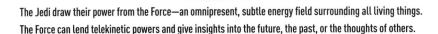

The Jedi draw their power from the Force—an omnipresent, subtle energy field surrounding all living things. The Force can lend telekinetic powers and give insights into the future, the past, or the thoughts of others.

THE JEDI HIGH COUNCIL

Saesee Tiin

The Iktotchi Saesee Tiin is one of the Jedi Order's greatest pilots, undertaking many missions in his personal starfighter, the *Sharp Spiral*. Tiin often joins Council debates after allowing his telepathic mind to race ahead and foresee possibilities.

Tough skin impervious to high winds of Iktotchon

Well-developed horns

Customary humanoid Jedi robes

THE TWELVE MEMBERS OF THE JEDI HIGH COUNCIL OVERSEE the activities of the Jedi Order, debating how to respond to galactic crises and meditating on the will of the Force. For nearly a thousand years, the Council has been composed of five lifetime members, four long-term members who serve until they choose to step down, and three limited-term members who sit for specified terms. This composition is intended to keep the Council wise and vigorous, with the chamber a place of open thought and speech, marked by mutual respect and shared purpose. Dissident Jedi such as Qui-Gon Jinn, however, argue that the Council has become insular and close-minded, more concerned with the Order's traditions and prerogatives than with ominous events in the Republic and strange stirrings in the Force.

The Chamber

From their chamber atop the southwestern spire of the Jedi Temple on Coruscant, the Jedi High Council can contemplate both Coruscant's teeming cityscape and the Temple's central spire—their ancient Order's most sacred place. The 12 council members sit in a ring formation around the chamber.

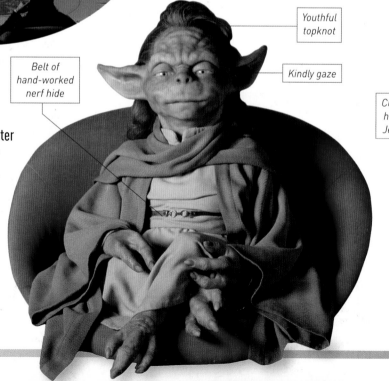

Youthful topknot

Kindly gaze

Belt of hand-worked nerf hide

Yaddle

Young at only 477, Jedi Master Yaddle achieved mastery of the Force through solitary meditation while imprisoned for more than a century on the planet Koba. Yaddle trained Council member Oppo Rancisis as a Padawan.

Yarael Poof

The attenuated Quermian Yarael Poof is the consummate master of Jedi mind tricks. He uses Force suggestions to bring conflicts to an abrupt end, turning combatants' own fears against themselves.

Quermian upper brain

Long neck for peering above low vegetation mats

Robe hides second set of arms and chest with lower brain

Large brain supported by second heart

Surcoat adapted from ancient Cerean garb

Lightsaber

Cerean cuffs

Plain trousers

Blade emitter

Blade power control

Tholothian tendrils

Traditional Quermian cannom collar

Gallia's second lightsaber replaces her first, which was destroyed on a mission

Utility pouch

Power cell access cap

UNORTHODOX JEDI
Adi Gallia sometimes uses her specialized lightsaber to perform the combat style Shien (Form V). The form employs a reverse grip, allowing for sweeping attacks.

Adi Gallia

Born into a highly placed diplomatic family stationed on Coruscant, Tholothian Jedi Adi Gallia's contacts within the Coruscant political machine make her one of Supreme Chancellor Valorum's most valuable intelligence sources. She is a good friend of Qui-Gon Jinn, and the two have teamed up on missions with their Padawans Siri Tachi and Obi-Wan Kenobi.

Jedi robe

Tall travel boots

Ki-Adi-Mundi

A Jedi Knight from the largely unspoiled paradise world of Cerea, Ki-Adi-Mundi's high-domed head holds a complex binary brain. A recent addition to the Council, he holds the rank of Master despite not having taken an apprentice.

SABER MASTER
Ki-Adi-Mundi is a master of the fast-paced Ataru form of lightsaber combat. In his role as Watchman of the Semagi sector, he uses his lightsaber skills to battle pirates and slavers.

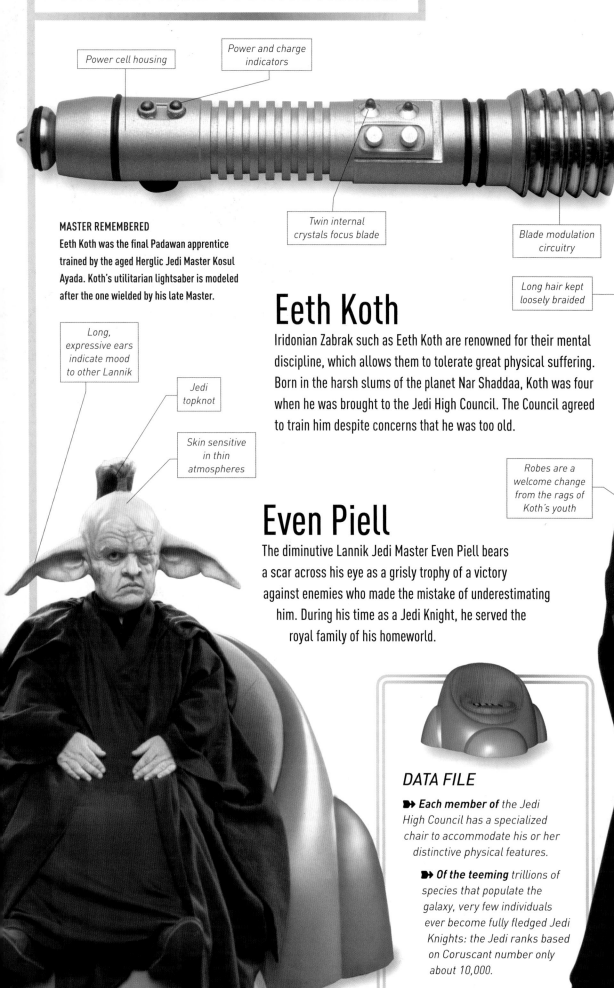

Power cell housing

Power and charge indicators

Vestigial horn patterns identify races of Iridonian Zabrak

Twin internal crystals focus blade

Blade modulation circuitry

Long hair kept loosely braided

MASTER REMEMBERED
Eeth Koth was the final Padawan apprentice trained by the aged Herglic Jedi Master Kosul Ayada. Koth's utilitarian lightsaber is modeled after the one wielded by his late Master.

Eeth Koth

Iridonian Zabrak such as Eeth Koth are renowned for their mental discipline, which allows them to tolerate great physical suffering. Born in the harsh slums of the planet Nar Shaddaa, Koth was four when he was brought to the Jedi High Council. The Council agreed to train him despite concerns that he was too old.

Robes are a welcome change from the rags of Koth's youth

Long, expressive ears indicate mood to other Lannik

Jedi topknot

Skin sensitive in thin atmospheres

Even Piell

The diminutive Lannik Jedi Master Even Piell bears a scar across his eye as a grisly trophy of a victory against enemies who made the mistake of underestimating him. During his time as a Jedi Knight, he served the royal family of his homeworld.

DATA FILE

➤ **Each member of** the Jedi High Council has a specialized chair to accommodate his or her distinctive physical features.

➤ **Of the teeming** trillions of species that populate the galaxy, very few individuals ever become fully fledged Jedi Knights: the Jedi ranks based on Coruscant number only about 10,000.

POISON AIR
Oxygen is corrosive to Kel Dor, who rely on goggles to protect their eyes when exposed to high concentrations.

Self-sealing eyepieces

Protective goggles

Antiox mask

Highly developed extrasensory organs

Mark of illumination

Plo Koon

A Kel Dor from Dorin, Plo Koon is equally skilled as a starfighter pilot and a lightsaber duelist. He has a rigid sense of right and wrong, and often urges the Jedi Council to bring justice to troubled Republic worlds.

Mask patterns are unique to Kel Dor clans

METAL MASK
Dorin's atmosphere is a mix of helium and dorinox. Kel Dor masks are handcrafted and often passed down within families.

Dense hair deters biting cygnats of Thisspias

Jaw can unhinge when eating

Depa Billaba

Adopting the traditional spiritual culture of Chalacta to honor her slain parents, Depa Billaba offers an ordered perspective to the wide-ranging minds of the Council. Her mentor, Mace Windu, has trained her in the dangerous lightsaber form Vaapad.

Razor-sharp claws

Muscular two-meter tail

Brown, Chalatan skintone

Oppo Rancisis

A master of military tactics, Oppo Rancisis was born into royalty on Thisspias. His mother, the planet's Blood Monarch, sent him to the Jedi for training, hoping he would return to claim the throne. But when the time came Oppo refused, instead choosing to remain a servant of the Republic and the Force on Coruscant.

QUI-GON JINN

MASTER QUI-GON JINN IS AN EXPERIENCED JEDI WHO HAS proven his value to the leadership of the Jedi Order in many important missions and difficult negotiations. In his maturity, however, he remains as restless as he was in his youth. When Qui-Gon encounters young Anakin Skywalker on the Outer Rim desert world of Tatooine, the Jedi is deeply struck by an unshakeable sense that the boy is part of the galaxy's destiny. In boldly championing the cause of Anakin, Qui-Gon sets in motion momentous events that will ultimately bring balance to the Force—but not without great cost.

Jedi robe

Qui-Gon is a capable diplomat and is respectful of those on the other side of the negotiating table, but he doesn't hesitate to use his reputation as a warrior to great effect, or drop the diplomatic niceties for blunt talk. Supreme Chancellor Valorum sends Qui-Gon to Naboo to strong-arm the Trade Federation into dropping its blockade—a mission the Senate knows nothing about.

Loyal to the Force

Qui-Gon has risen to prominence within the Jedi Order, and is well-known to the High Council membership. In spite of his outstanding service as a Jedi Knight and Master, however, he has been passed over for a seat on the Council. This is due to his bold, headstrong nature and his insistence on knowing and heeding the will of the Force in all situations, even when that causes him to defy his Jedi peers and elders to follow his own path.

Jedi tunic

Hook for sliding down cables

Force Limits

Jedi are capable of amazing feats of agility and strength, but even they must carry some field gear. As part of his essential kit, Qui-Gon carries a multi-purpose hook launcher with a liquid-cable rotator.

Qui-Gon and Obi-Wan travel to Naboo expecting nothing more than a shipboard conference, but fortunately they come prepared for unexpected contingencies. Their Jedi field gear is put to use when they are forced to negotiate the fast-flowing waters of a Naboo waterfall.

Liquid-cable reservoir

Dual-strand liquid-cable rotator

Spinner tip

JEDI FIELD GEAR

Grappling spike launcher

Rugged travel boots

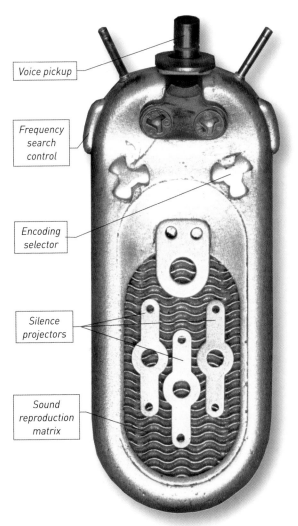

Voice pickup

Frequency search control

Encoding selector

Silence projectors

Sound reproduction matrix

Reception antenna

COMLINK REVERSE VIEW

Inert plaeklite casing

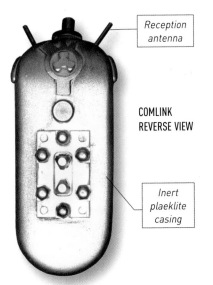
Comlink

Qui-Gon's miniature comlink allows him to keep in touch with Obi-Wan Kenobi when the two operate separately. It features complex security devices to prevent unauthorized interception and is unlabeled to thwart use by non-Jedi. A silence projector lends privacy to conversations and helps Qui-Gon maintain stealth in the field.

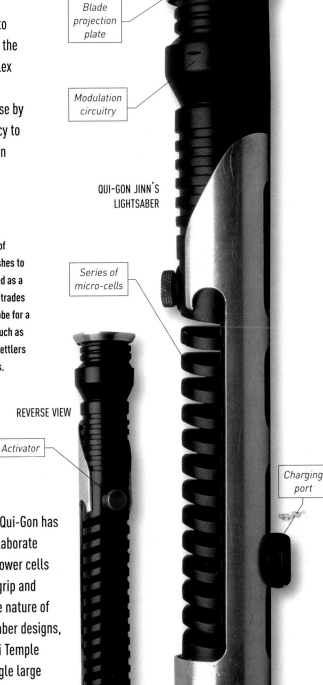

Blade projection plate

Modulation circuitry

QUI-GON JINN'S LIGHTSABER

Series of micro-cells

REVERSE VIEW

Activator

Charging port

LOW-KEY JEDI
On the desert planet of Tatooine, Qui-Gon wishes to avoid being recognized as a Jedi. Accordingly, he trades his customary Jedi robe for a rough-spun poncho such as those worn by local settlers and moisture farmers.

On Tatooine, Qui-Gon battles a Sith warrior wielding a deadly lightsaber. Since lightsabers are seldom handled by non-Jedi, the Order primarily uses them as a defense against blaster bolts rather than other lightsabers. However, lightsaber dueling is taught as part of classical Jedi training.

Lightsaber

Following the custom of his day, Qui-Gon has built a lightsaber with a highly elaborate internal design. Multiple small power cells are stored in the scalloped handgrip and microscopic circuitry governs the nature of the energy blade. Simpler lightsaber designs, built outside the halls of the Jedi Temple on Coruscant, typically use a single large power cell inside a solid handgrip.

TOYDARIAN TROUBLE

Some species are naturally immune to the Jedi mind tricks of all but the most powerful Masters. Qui-Gon Jinn has never dealt with a Toydarian before his encounter with Watto on Tatooine, and soon finds that he needs more than Force-assisted "suggestions" to persuade the hovering junk dealer to cooperate with him.

Qui-Gon loads his holoprojector with selected images from the technical databanks onboard the Naboo Royal Starship. He intends to use them to help obtain repair parts when the ship is grounded on Tatooine.

Holoprojector

One of the utility devices that Qui-Gon carries is a small holoprojector. This can be tuned with a comlink to carry a hologram transmission for face-to-face contact, or it can be used as an independent image recorder and projector.

Projection platform

Tines rotate downward to plug into signal feed or to link to larger image projector

Sturdy construction for field use

Casing ring

Qui-Gon is convinced that Anakin is the Chosen One predicted by an ancient Jedi prophecy—the individual who will restore balance to the Force. Certain that their meeting was the will of the Force, he is determined to train Anakin as a Jedi. But the High Council refuses his request. They doubt the prophecy and sense danger in the boy.

Qui-Gon earned the rank of Master when he trained his first Padawan apprentice to Knighthood, although his second apprentice failed to become a Knight. Obi-Wan is Qui-Gon's third Padawan and a worthy student of his wisdom and skill.

DATA FILE

▶▶ *The funeral of a* Jedi *is generally a simple affair: The Jedi Code warns against emotional attachments, which include mourning or missing the dead after they have become one with the Force.*

Jedi Test

Qui-Gon takes a blood sample from Anakin and transmits the profile to Obi-Wan, who tests the sample's levels of midi-chlorians: symbiotic microbes that allow beings to feel and use the Force. Anakin's levels are higher than those of any known Jedi, leaving Qui-Gon even more certain that this lowly Tatooine slave boy is the Chosen One whose destiny will reshape the galaxy.

Test phase indicator screens

Lid hides culture test chamber

Data port

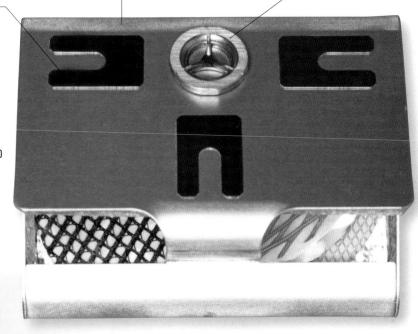

JEDI BLOOD
TEST KIT

Antibacterial lining

Midi-chlorian reactant cleansing swab

Jedi test kits employ swabs treated with a chemical that reacts to midi-chlorians. A being's midi-chlorian count indicates his or her Force potential.

Chemically neutral cleansing swab

INTERIOR VIEW

Long hair worn back to keep vision clear

Saber held to parry slash

DUEL ON NABOO
After crossing sabers on Tatooine, Qui-Gon and Darth Maul meet again in the Theed Generator Complex. The tattooed warrior is strong in the Sith arts, using his fury to give his attacks a terrifying strength. Mortally wounded, Qui-Gon uses his last breath to beg Obi-Wan to train Anakin as a Jedi.

OBI-WAN KENOBI

OBI-WAN KENOBI HAS FOLLOWED A RESPONSIBLE PATH ON HIS journey toward Jedi knighthood as the Padawan apprentice to Jedi Master Qui-Gon Jinn. Strongly influenced by other leading Jedi as well as by Qui-Gon, Obi-Wan is more brooding and cautious than his teacher. He is careful to weigh the consequences of his actions and is reluctant to entangle himself unnecessarily in transgressions against the will of the Jedi High Council. A serious, quiet man possessed of a dry sense of humor, Obi-Wan strives to be worthy of his order and feels honored to be Qui-Gon's student, although he worries about his Master's tendency to take risks in defiance of the Council. Nevertheless, Obi-Wan follows Qui-Gon Jinn's example and develops an independent spirit of his own.

Short hair of a Padawan apprentice

Tunic

Hooded robe

Belt fastener

Fastener band

Apprentice's long braid

UTILITY BELT

Utility belt

Traditional leather

Food and tool pouches

BREATHER POUCH

UTILITY POUCHES
On field missions, Jedi carry a basic kit consisting of medical supplies, multitools, and other essential devices.

Jedi Gear

The basic Jedi clothing of belted tunic, travel boots, and robe speaks of the simplicity vested in Jedi philosophy and carries overtones of their mission as travelers. Individual Jedi keep utility belt field gear to a minimum. As initiates are taught in the great Temple, Jedi reputations are based on their spirits and not on material trappings.

Energy capsule

Dispenser track

Travel clip

FOOD AND ENERGY CAPSULES
Jedi are encouraged to sample local cuisine, as many cultures share food as a sign of good fellowship. However, on some missions it is simpler to get sustenance from concentrated capsules.

Food capsule

Rugged travel boots

A99 Aquata Breather

In this era, Jedi Knights usually carry various high-tech devices concealed in their robes or in belt pouches. On their mission to Naboo, Obi-Wan and Qui-Gon Jinn carry A99 Aquata breathers, knowing that much of the planet's surface is water. Breathers allow the Jedi to survive underwater for up to two hours. In other times, Jedi have avoided such technological devices in order to minimize their dependence on anything but their own resourcefulness.

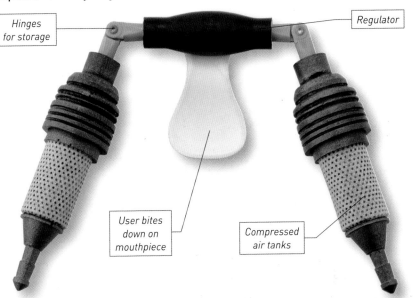

Hinges for storage

Regulator

User bites down on mouthpiece

Compressed air tanks

Atmospheric sensors

Variable airflow feeder

SIDE VIEW

The A99's sensors instantly analyze conditions and optimize the breather's functions for use in different atmospheric pressures, underwater, or in a vacuum.

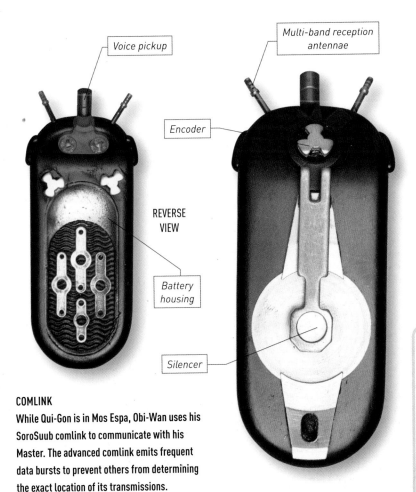

Voice pickup

Multi-band reception antennae

Encoder

REVERSE VIEW

Battery housing

Silencer

COMLINK
While Qui-Gon is in Mos Espa, Obi-Wan uses his SoroSuub comlink to communicate with his Master. The advanced comlink emits frequent data bursts to prevent others from determining the exact location of its transmissions.

Hyperdrive

When the hyperdrive generator of the Naboo Royal Starship is damaged, Obi-Wan stays on board to look after the drive core while Qui-Gon seeks a replacement generator in Mos Espa on Tatooine. Constantly monitoring the damaged component, Obi-Wan readies the core for repairs.

DATA FILE

➤ *Jedi robes are virtually* indistinguishable from the simple robes worn by many species throughout the galaxy. This signifies the Jedi pledge to the service and protection of even the most humble galactic citizen.

➤ *Obi-Wan remains* loyal to Qui-Gon even when this puts him at odds with the Jedi High Council.

Padawan's Progress

Obi-Wan still has lessons to learn before he is ready to become a Jedi Knight: He often lets his anxieties distract him from feeling the will of the Force, and he is still careless in the way all young people can be, particularly when it comes to handling his lightsaber. But Qui-Gon is confident his Padawan will overcome these obstacles, and acknowledges his skills: Obi-Wan has the makings of a fine diplomat and duelist.

Centered awareness

Eyes scan opponents

Neutral stance can easily shift to parry or sweep attack

Hooded robe removed for intense combat

Loose-fitting pants allow freedom of movement

Battle stance

Faced with the mechanized minions of the Trade Federation droid army, Obi-Wan knows that he need not exercise the combat restraint he would use with living beings. He puts his fight training to good use, yet maintains cool concentration.

ACCEPTING AN APPRENTICE
Obi-Wan Kenobi views Anakin Skywalker as an unnecessary risk, both as a travel companion and as a potential Jedi. But at Qui-Gon Jinn's request, Obi-Wan puts his concerns aside and accepts Anakin as his apprentice, beginning a long and fateful relationship.

DATA FILE

▸▸ **Born on the planet** Stewjon, Obi-Wan was initially rejected for training as a Padawan and was headed for a career in the AgriCorps. He was sent to a mining colony on the planet Bandomeer.

▸▸ **The Jedi High Council** bestows on Obi-Wan the title of Jedi Knight after he proves himself in a duel with the Sith Lord Darth Maul.

DANGEROUS DUEL

Obi-Wan is an exceptional lightsaber duelist and a formidable opponent for Darth Maul. The Sith Lord fights with inhuman intensity, fueled by the hateful energy of the dark side of the Force. In the heat of mortal combat and on the brink of death, Obi-Wan faces the temptation to draw on the same terrible strength in order to defeat his enemy.

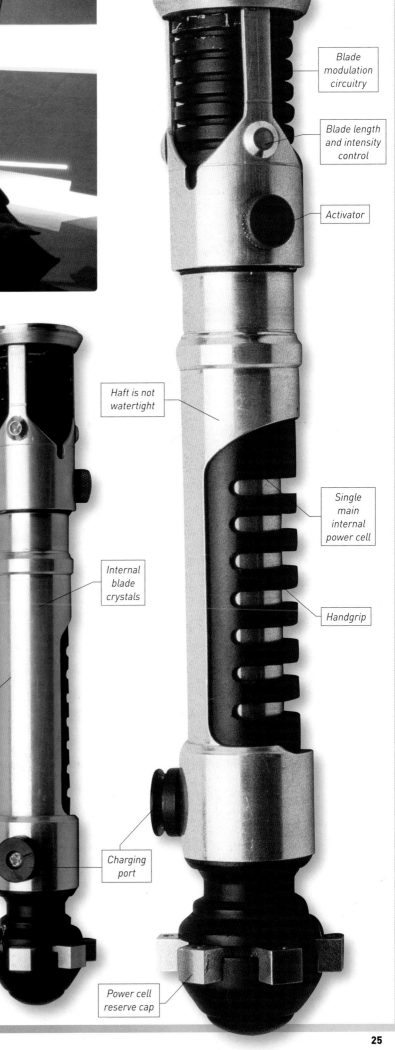

Blade modulation circuitry

Blade length and intensity control

Activator

Haft is not watertight

Single main internal power cell

Handgrip

Charging port

Power cell reserve cap

Blade emitter

Internal blade crystals

Design recalls Qui-Gon's saber

Obi-Wan and Darth Maul duel within the heart of Theed Palace's immense Generator Complex, their anger and intensity an echo of the roiling, energized plasma coursing through the generator's innards. All looks lost for Obi-Wan when Maul knocks him into a pit leading to the plasma core, leaving the young Jedi clinging to a security beacon inside the fathomless shaft.

Lightsaber

Lightsabers follow a common design. Optional elements, like blade power and length modulators, are small and unobtrusive. Accordingly, Jedi lightsabers appear similar at first glance. A closer inspection, however, reveals that lightsabers rarely look exactly alike. All are hand-built by the initiates themselves, making design details a matter of individual choice. Most Padawan apprentices build their lightsabers to resemble those of their teachers as a mark of respect.

THE NEIMOIDIANS

RAISED AS GRUBS UNTIL THE AGE OF SEVEN, YOUNG NEIMOIDIANS are kept in communal hives and given limited amounts of food. The less acquisitive ones are allowed to die as others hoard more than they can eat. This practice makes Neimoidians greedy and fearful of death. As adults, Neimoidians are known for their exceptional organizing abilities. Driven by their intense desire for possessions, they have built the largest commercial corporation in the galaxy. Led by Neimoidians, the Trade Federation is a labyrinthine organization of bureaucrats and trade officials from many worlds that has insinuated itself throughout the galaxy.

Neimoidian senatorial miter

Ferrous pigmented sclera

NEIMOIDIAN SHUTTLE
Recalling the body shapes of giant domesticated beetles on Neimoidia, the Neimoidian shuttle conveys trade officers from orbiting freighters to planet surfaces and the hangars of other vessels. The pointed landing claws are only effective on hard surfaces, because Neimoidians are not interested in landing on bare fields.

Lott Dod

The Trade Federation is so powerful that it is represented in the Galactic Senate—an ominous situation. Its senator, Lott Dod, uses bureaucratic lies and procedural tricks to further Trade Federation aims from his Senate seat. Even Dod, however, is unable to thwart the new taxes that threaten to cut into Trade Federation profits.

Supreme representative mantle

Insincere gesture of innocence

Insanely expensive Tyrian violet cloth

Diplomatic ploov

Financial officer's collar

SHUTTLE AIRLOCK STERILIZING MODULE

Antiseptic gas nozzle

Degreasing compound mister

Heavy deflector-shield gear

Cockpit is sealed since shuttle is piloted entirely by instruments

Lounge in center

Generator vents

Landing gear flexure equipment

Pointed claws imitate those of living beetles

Outer hatch (open)

Boarding ramp

NEIMOIDIAN SHUTTLE PASSENGER SECTION

NEIMOIDIAN DRESS
In status-obsessed Neimoidian society, elaborate clothing asserts the wearer's wealth and social position over other jealous Neimoidians. Hats, cloaks, and drapes, as well as colors and fabrics, all have particular symbolic meanings.

Rune Haako

As Settlement Officer of the Trade Federation armed forces, Rune Haako serves as diplomatic attaché and legal counsel to Nute Gunray. Haako has a reputation for ruthlessly treating business partners as adversaries and conniving to wrest every last credit from them.

Neimoidians are cautious by nature and the Trade Federation has always been careful to hide its acts of extortion and manipulation behind lies and protests of good faith. Their open aggression against Naboo is new territory for them, and both Gunray and Haako are uneasy about the possibility of escalation.

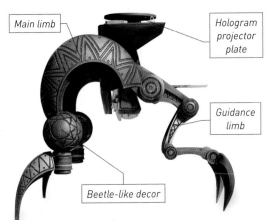

Main limb

Hologram projector plate

Guidance limb

Beetle-like decor

MECHNO-CHAIR
Walking mechno-chairs are neither comfortable nor practical. However, they are hugely expensive and express the high status of their user. They also serve as platforms for hologram transmissions of high-ranking individuals.

Attorney's cowl

Nute Gunray

A Commanding Viceroy of the Trade Federation, Nute Gunray wields great authority and serves on the Trade Federation Executive Board. Deceitful and willing to kill for his far-reaching commercial aims, Gunray directs the actions of the secret army fleet from the bridge of the flagship.

Viceroy's crested tiara

Wheedling expression

Viceroy's collar

Underhanded gesture

DATA FILE

➡ **The Neimoidians' organizational** skills come from running mass hives and vast fungus farms on their home world of Neimoidia.

➡ **Trade Federation freighters**, hauling cargo between the far-flung stars of the Republic, are a familiar sight in orbit above many civilized worlds.

THE FLAGSHIP CREW

Data goggles allow pilot to see constant holographic data readouts

WHEN THE BLOCKADE FAILS TO INTIMIDATE THE NABOO
Queen into submission, the Trade Federation prepares for the next step: invasion. The Sith Lord Darth Sidious commands Neimoidian Viceroy Nute Gunray to order the deployment of an immense secret army hidden in the cargo hangars of converted trade freighters. The plans proceed under the direction of Daultay Dofine, captain of the command vessel *Saak'ak*. Dofine and his crews are used to running Trade Federation convoys, not military units, but Sidious has assured Gunray that their lack of experience is unimportant. He promises that the Trade Federation's invasion will meet little resistance on Naboo or in the Senate.

Vessel command officer's miter

Skin mottled from self-indulgence

Comlink

Daultay Dofine reports to Neimoidian Viceroy Nute Gunray—but worries more about Gunray reporting to Darth Sidious.

Daultay Dofine

Captain of the Trade Federation's flagship vessel, Daultay Dofine has climbed the ladder of rank through a combination of high birth, back-stabbing, and groveling behavior toward his superiors. Nevertheless, Dofine finds the bold plans of the Sith Lord Darth Sidious too dangerous for his tastes. However, he soon learns that his tastes are entirely irrelevant.

Neimoidian pilots and communications officers wear data goggles that are wired directly into their brains, allowing them to monitor, activate, and deactivate starship control systems with their thoughts.

Monitor displays complex star weather systems

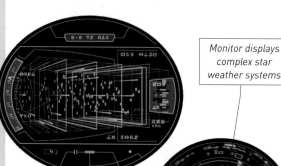

Commanders consider cybernetic implants beneath them, relying instead on monitors.

DATA FILE

➤➤ **The Trade Federation** has proved able to defend trade routes against bandits, but blockading a Republic system is a big test of their mettle.

➤➤ **The wealthy, arrogant** Neimoidians tend to avoid any kind of labor, preferring to use droids instead.

Protocol droid TC-14 ignores the foul play brewing against the Jedi ambassadors for the Supreme Chancellor. When the Jedi visitors are hit with poison gas, TC-14 simply wants to get out of the way, apologizing even to the battle droids outside the meeting room.

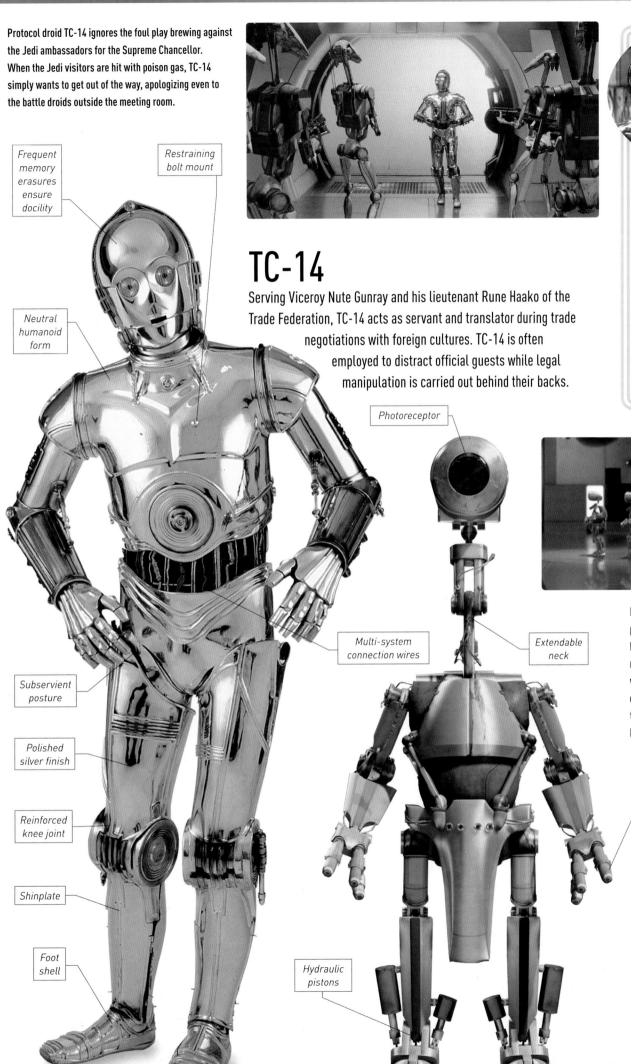

Frequent memory erasures ensure docility

Restraining bolt mount

Neutral humanoid form

Subservient posture

Polished silver finish

Reinforced knee joint

Shinplate

Foot shell

TC-14

Serving Viceroy Nute Gunray and his lieutenant Rune Haako of the Trade Federation, TC-14 acts as servant and translator during trade negotiations with foreign cultures. TC-14 is often employed to distract official guests while legal manipulation is carried out behind their backs.

Photoreceptor

Multi-system connection wires

Extendable neck

Hydraulic pistons

Simple manipulators

DATA FILE

➡ **The TC series of** protocol droids is nearly identical to Cybot Galactica's better-known 3PO-series, but uses the new and more powerful TranLangIII Communicator module.

➡ **Ancient galactic tradition,** which is hotly debated on some worlds, assigns feminine programming to most protocol droids in diplomatic service.

PK droids aren't smart, but that's not their purpose: They're cheap labor programmed by higher-order droids to execute simple, repetitive tasks. If not given frequent memory wipes, PK droids can become resentful of their droid superiors and organic masters, muttering to each other about the unfairness of life at the bottom of the droid heap.

PK Droids

Manufactured by the ancient megacorp Cybot Galactica, PK-series worker droids are common sights in spaceports and on starships across the galaxy, handling a vast number of mundane jobs. Organics and more advanced droids rarely deign to notice them as they follow their routines.

THE INVASION FORCE

Ion engines

Foot ramp

Wingtip blaster cannons

Landing Ships

A fleet of specially built C-9979 craft land the Trade Federation invasion force on Naboo. These landing craft are built to hold heavy armor and legions of troops in their bodies and repulsorlift wings. Groups of three landing craft are deployed in a pattern that cuts off all the Naboo cities from each other.

AFTER JAMMING ALL COMMUNICATIONS ON NABOO, the Trade Federation begins its invasion of the pacifist planet. Massive landing ships descend into the forests, their bellies filled with vast numbers of droid troops and powerful war machines. From the landing ships emerge hulking MTT troop carriers, smashing through trees to ferry battle droids to their coordinated muster points. AATs also move out, gun turrets scanning for any signs of resistance. And high above, droid starfighters lurk at the edge of space, on guard against any counterattack.

Control room

Asked to create a landing craft for the armies of the Trade Federation, the Haor Chall Engineering works adapted the design of commercial cargo barges used by the Trade Federation's merchant fleet. The huge double wings contain garages for MTTs and AATs, which deploy from a foot ramp when the craft lands.

Droid rack extending

MTT

Designed by Baktoid Armor Workshop, the Multi-Troop Transport can batter down walls with its armored prow and quartet of blaster cannons. The MTT then opens its main hatch and extends out a rack holding 112 battle droid soldiers, all folded up in their space-saving configuration.

Lower deployment hatch

Heavy armor plating

Droid deployment hatch

Twin blaster cannons

Repulsorlift impellors

Power generators

Dispatched to strategic positions, MTTs thunder along routes programmed by their droid pilots. The generator's exhaust and coolant is vented down toward the ground, creating a howling windstorm.

The troop transports' vital equipment—such as reactors and main engines—are located at the rear to give them greater protection. Trade Federation strategy also calls for each MTT to be protected by a pair of AATs.

Repulsorlift exhaust system

UNDERSIDE VIEW

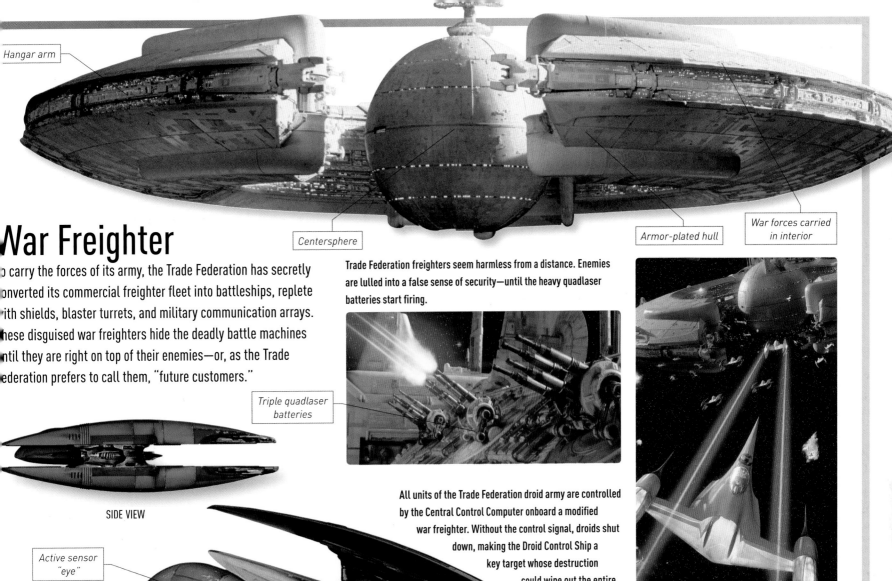

Hangar arm

Centersphere

Armor-plated hull

War forces carried in interior

War Freighter

To carry the forces of its army, the Trade Federation has secretly converted its commercial freighter fleet into battleships, replete with shields, blaster turrets, and military communication arrays. These disguised war freighters hide the deadly battle machines until they are right on top of their enemies—or, as the Trade Federation prefers to call them, "future customers."

Trade Federation freighters seem harmless from a distance. Enemies are lulled into a false sense of security—until the heavy quadlaser batteries start firing.

Triple quadlaser batteries

SIDE VIEW

All units of the Trade Federation droid army are controlled by the Central Control Computer onboard a modified war freighter. Without the control signal, droids shut down, making the Droid Control Ship a key target whose destruction could wipe out the entire invasion force.

Droid fighters follow only a few simple attack patterns, relying on superior numbers to overwhelm foes.

Active sensor "eye"

Walking wing in attack mode

Torpedo firing channels

Droid Starfighter

The complex, precision-engineered droid starfighters built for the Trade Federation by the Xi Char cathedral factories are variable-geometry machines. The long, wing-like claws open to reveal deadly laser cannons. On the ground, these "wings" become movable legs as the fighter shifts to walk mode for surface patrol.

Flight assault lasers

Walking limbtips

AAT

Baktoid's Armored Assault Tanks bristle with weaponry, carrying laser cannons and a variety of explosive shells. Four battle droids make up a tank crew.

DATA FILE

➤ **Droid starfighters are** known as "Vulture droids" because of their ungainly stride in walk mode.

➤ **Trade Federation ships** are built around centerspheres, which can function as ships in their own right.

WALK MODE

BATTLE DROIDS

THE GALACTIC REPUBLIC HAS SURVIVED DISAGREEMENTS, standoffs, and even rebellion among its many member worlds, relying on the Jedi Knights to quell conflicts. In this enlightened age, few standing armies are maintained that serve anything other than ceremonial purposes, since an army could be regarded as an open threat to galactic peace. Nevertheless, as the bureaucracy of the Republic Senate indulges in endless debates and procedural bickering, the use of force has become a real threat. The wealthy Trade Federation has quietly gone far beyond any other group in assembling a massive army composed of ghostly, emotionless droid soldiers that are ready to do their masters' bidding without a touch of emotion or mercy. Their deployment upon the peaceful people of Naboo heralds the end of an age of peace and security in the galaxy.

Droid Army

Battle droids are thinly armored, lack effective audiovisual sensors, and are poor shots. But these flaws matter little when compared to their one great advantage: They are cheap to manufacture. With minimal lead time, Trade Federation factories can produce these droids in staggering numbers.

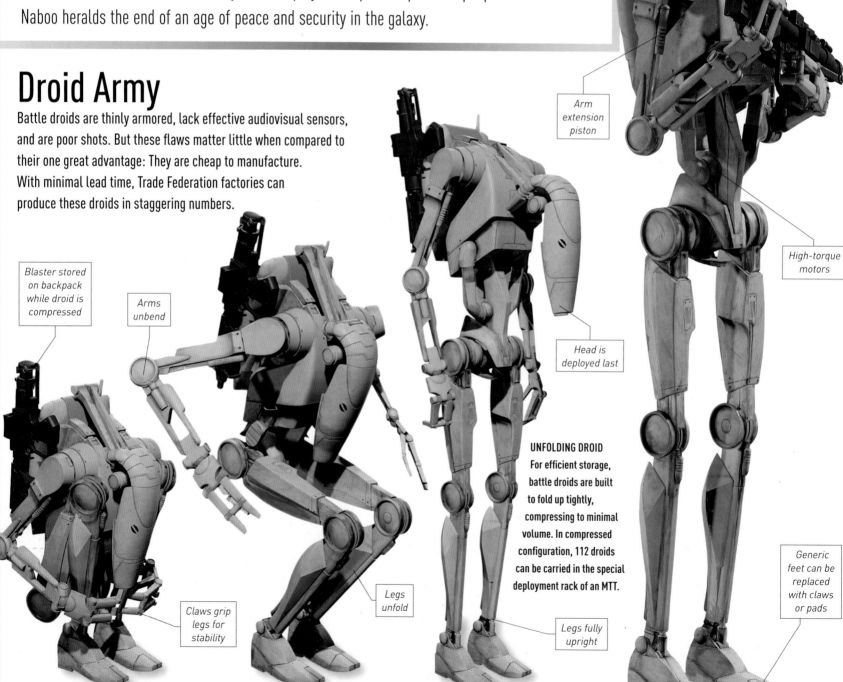

Signal reception boost antenna

General command storage

Specialized movement processor

Transmitter boost antenna

Optical sensor

Sampled movement cycle memory

Signal boost and power augment backpack

Arm extension piston

High-torque motors

Blaster stored on backpack while droid is compressed

Arms unbend

Head is deployed last

UNFOLDING DROID
For efficient storage, battle droids are built to fold up tightly, compressing to minimal volume. In compressed configuration, 112 droids can be carried in the special deployment rack of an MTT.

Legs unfold

Claws grip legs for stability

Legs fully upright

Generic feet can be replaced with claws or pads

Battle Droid Head

The battle droid head, lacking a brain of its own, contains little more than a large and sensitive control signal receiver. Small processors collect movement and limited sensory data for transmission back to the Central Control Computer, and a vocoder enables the droid to talk.

IN THEIR IMAGE

With their long heads and spindly bodies, battle droids resemble mechanical versions of the Geonosians who designed them. But many Neimoidians believe the droids are designed to resemble Neimoidian skeletons—an image of death that makes them seem more threatening.

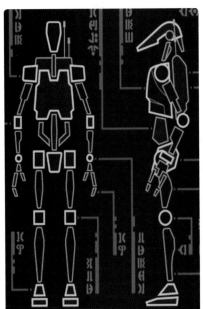

Receiver assembly casing

Signal transmission lines

Dephasing anticode sieve

Code processing baffles

Override signal receptor

Signal receiver assembly

Speech processor

Sensory input cable

Signal clarifier septode

Magnetic stabilizing field bar

Signal confirmation module

Speech transmission lines

Interference dissipator mat

Stored vocabulary triggered by control impulses

Vocoder

RISE AND SHINE

A commander on the ground generally gives the word for battle droids to unfold and deploy, but the distant Central Control Computer relays that order to individual droid units.

Battle Droid Blaster

Since battle droids are capable of wielding deadly blasters, they are designed to be incapable of independent thought. They are governed entirely by the Central Control Computer and have no ability to react to surprises or learn from experience. While battle droids can be deadly, their firing accuracy is poor.

In combat, battle droids follow simple attack and defense patterns optimized for squads of eight mechanicals.

DATA FILE

➤➤ **Their lack of independent** thought processors make battle droids immune to fear, cowardice, or mercy pleas.

➤➤ **The smooth movements** of battle droids are the result of pre-digitized motion-capture data taken from live soldiers and broadcast by the Central Control Computer to each droid.

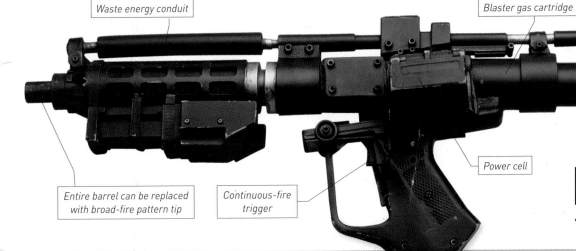

Waste energy conduit

Blaster gas cartridge

Power cell

Entire barrel can be replaced with broad-fire pattern tip

Continuous-fire trigger

IDENTIFICATION NUMBERS

Galactic basic numerals identify individual droids, but Trade Federation central computers can track each deployed droid without them. The numbers are there to assist organic droid commanders on the battlefield.

1 2 3 4 5 6 7 8 9

PAC

The droid rack used inside the MTT can be adapted for mounting an unarmed repulsorlift cargo sled. Like MTTs, Platoon Attack Craft carry 112 droids in a space-saving, racked configuration. A pair of pilot battle droids drives each PAC into its designated deployment zones.

Multispectrum headlamp

Drive unit

Droid rack

Landing skids

Control yoke

PAC PROTECTION
With no weapons of their own, PACs rely heavily on AATs, STAPs, and other Trade Federation war craft for protection when transporting droids into the field of battle.

Battle droid scouts and antipersonnel clean-up snipers are swept through the air on Single Trooper Aerial Platforms armed with twin blasters. The open design of the STAP means the droid pilot rides exposed to enemy fire, relying on the vehicle's speed and agility to defeat opponents.

Twin blasters

STAP

A military variant of the civilian "airhook" used in many parts of the galaxy, the Single Trooper Aerial Platform is designed for recon and scouting missions. Battle droids aren't bothered by turbine exhaust or G-forces, so the STAP is lighter and faster than civilian airhooks. The repulsorlift STAP's minimal structure allows it to thread its way through dense, difficult terrain that would be inaccessible to larger vehicles.

Power cell housing

Antigravity projector

Blaster function controls

Drive turbine

Footlock

Foot panel

REAR VIEW

OFFICER'S MACROBINOCULARS

To save on costs, the Trade Federation opted not to build battle droids with advanced audiovisual capabilities—their eyesight is comparable to that of many organics. Command droids such as OOM-9 use macrobinoculars to scan areas for enemy units.

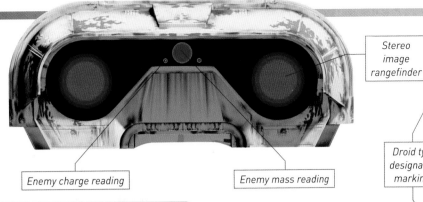

Enemy charge reading

Enemy mass reading

Stereo image rangefinder

Droid type designation markings

Power backpack

Security battle droids are decorated with red markings. They typically keep order as guards aboard starships, working in squads overseen by a command officer droid.

Emblazoned in blue, pilot droids rarely stray from vehicle control rooms or starship bridges, and their specialized subroutines make them all but useless if pressed into service as infantry.

Command Officer

In order to streamline communication between Trade Federation officials and droid troops, certain battle droids, such as OOM-9, are designated Command Officers. Orders are conveyed to officer droids via priority channels from the Central Control Computer processors, but their advanced cognitive units allow them to think independently.

Macrobinoculars

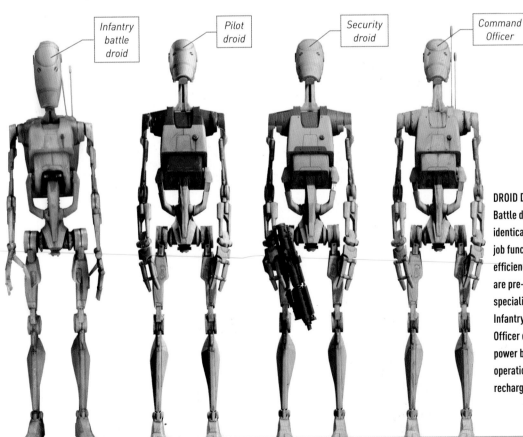

Infantry battle droid

Pilot droid

Security droid

Command Officer

OOM-9

DROID DESIGNATIONS

Battle droids are structurally identical irrespective of job function. To increase efficiency, however, droids are pre-programmed with specialized subroutines. Infantry and Command Officer droids are fitted with power backpacks to boost operational range and extend recharge intervals.

DROIDEKAS

TO MAKE UP FOR THE WEAKNESSES OF BATTLE DROIDS, a special contract was awarded for the creation of an altogether different combat droid that would be a much more serious weapon. The design was created by a species of chitinous Colicoids in their own image on a planet far from the Republic's core. Colicoids are known for their completely unfeeling and murderous ways, and Colla IV has been embroiled for many years in diplomatic disputes related to the death and consumption of visitors to the system. The droideka was exactly what concerned Trade Federation officers wanted: a formidable, heavy-duty killing machine to back up the battle droids in the face of determined opposition.

DATA FILE

▶▶ *Like battle droids*, droidekas lack independent logic processors and are run by signals from the Central Control Computer. The Colicoids dislike this system and have built custom droidekas equipped with computer brains.

▶▶ *Droidekas are commonly* known as destroyer droids in many parts of the galaxy.

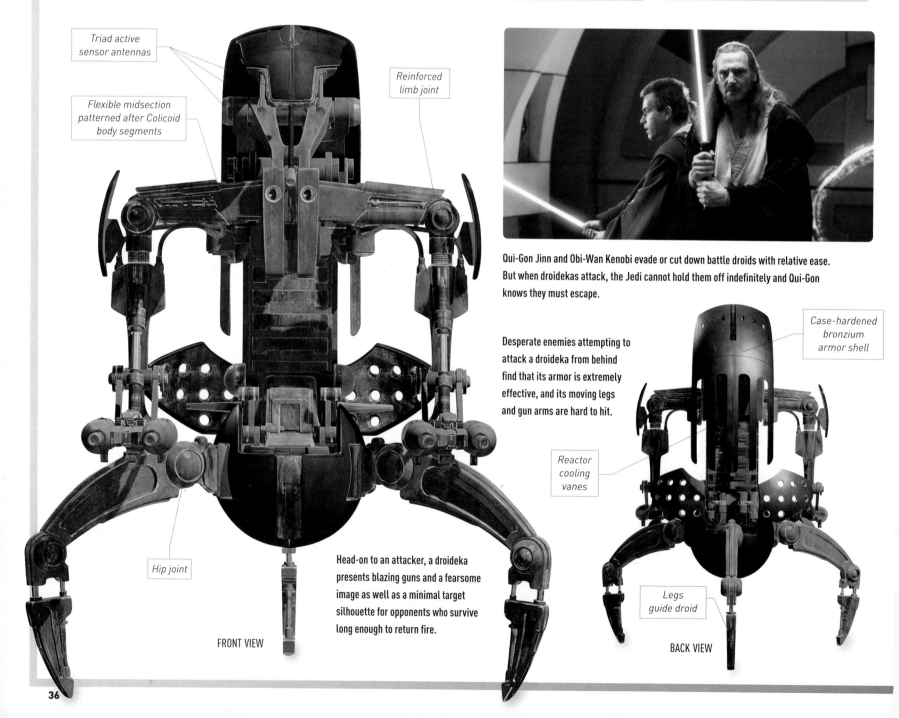

Triad active sensor antennas

Flexible midsection patterned after Colicoid body segments

Reinforced limb joint

Qui-Gon Jinn and Obi-Wan Kenobi evade or cut down battle droids with relative ease. But when droidekas attack, the Jedi cannot hold them off indefinitely and Qui-Gon knows they must escape.

Desperate enemies attempting to attack a droideka from behind find that its armor is extremely effective, and its moving legs and gun arms are hard to hit.

Case-hardened bronzium armor shell

Reactor cooling vanes

Hip joint

Head-on to an attacker, a droideka presents blazing guns and a fearsome image as well as a minimal target silhouette for opponents who survive long enough to return fire.

FRONT VIEW

Legs guide droid

BACK VIEW

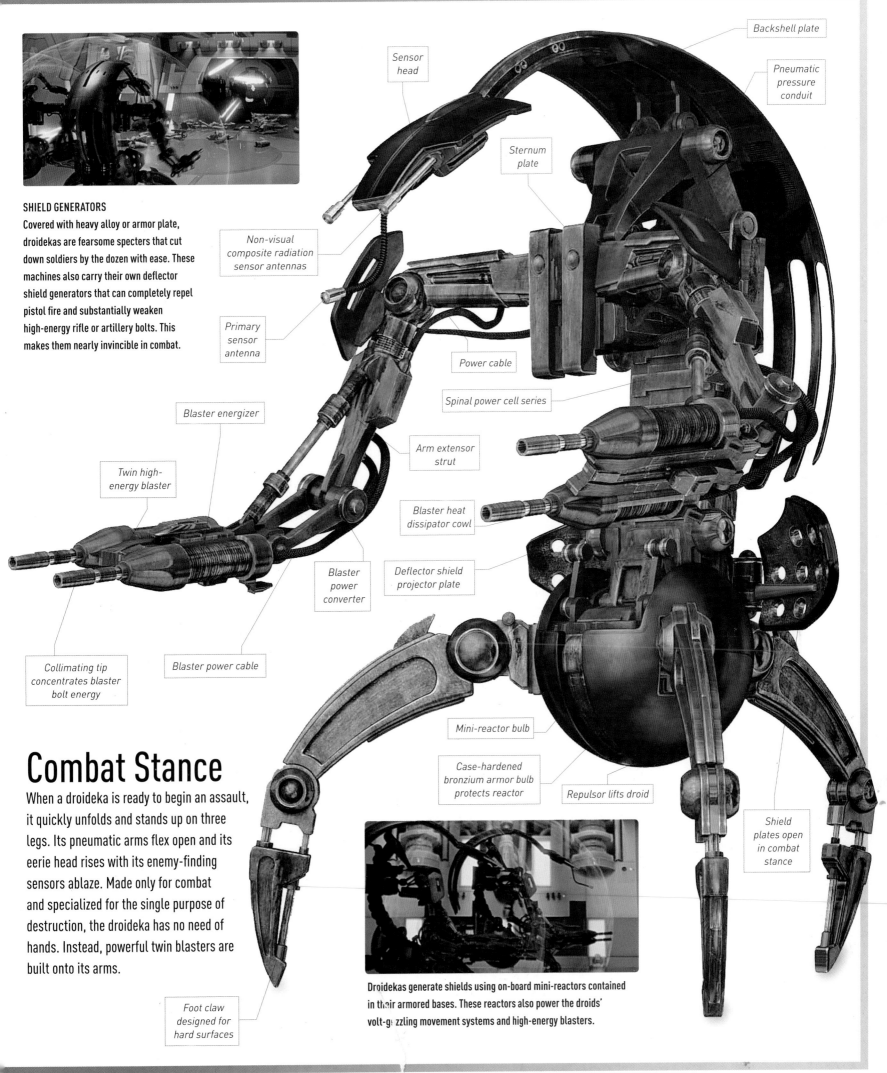

SHIELD GENERATORS

Covered with heavy alloy or armor plate, droidekas are fearsome specters that cut down soldiers by the dozen with ease. These machines also carry their own deflector shield generators that can completely repel pistol fire and substantially weaken high-energy rifle or artillery bolts. This makes them nearly invincible in combat.

Backshell plate

Pneumatic pressure conduit

Sensor head

Sternum plate

Non-visual composite radiation sensor antennas

Power cable

Primary sensor antenna

Spinal power cell series

Blaster energizer

Arm extensor strut

Twin high-energy blaster

Blaster heat dissipator cowl

Blaster power converter

Deflector shield projector plate

Collimating tip concentrates blaster bolt energy

Blaster power cable

Mini-reactor bulb

Case-hardened bronzium armor bulb protects reactor

Repulsor lifts droid

Shield plates open in combat stance

Combat Stance

When a droideka is ready to begin an assault, it quickly unfolds and stands up on three legs. Its pneumatic arms flex open and its eerie head rises with its enemy-finding sensors ablaze. Made only for combat and specialized for the single purpose of destruction, the droideka has no need of hands. Instead, powerful twin blasters are built onto its arms.

Foot claw designed for hard surfaces

Droidekas generate shields using on-board mini-reactors contained in their armored bases. These reactors also power the droids' volt-guzzling movement systems and high-energy blasters.

Wheel Form

For compact storage and optimum travel speed, droidekas retract into the shape of a wheel. Using pulsed internal micro-repulsors in sequence, they roll themselves into battle, opening at the last moment into their combat form. In transit, the wheel mode presents a smaller and faster target to enemy gunfire, with the droideka's weapons and systems defended by its limbs and shell.

Backshell plate protects weapons while droideka is rolling toward enemy

During the Great Grass Plains Battle on Naboo, the Gungans hope the uneven terrain will slow the droidekas' advance in wheel form. But the plains prove uniform enough that the droids roll through the shield perimeter with relative ease.

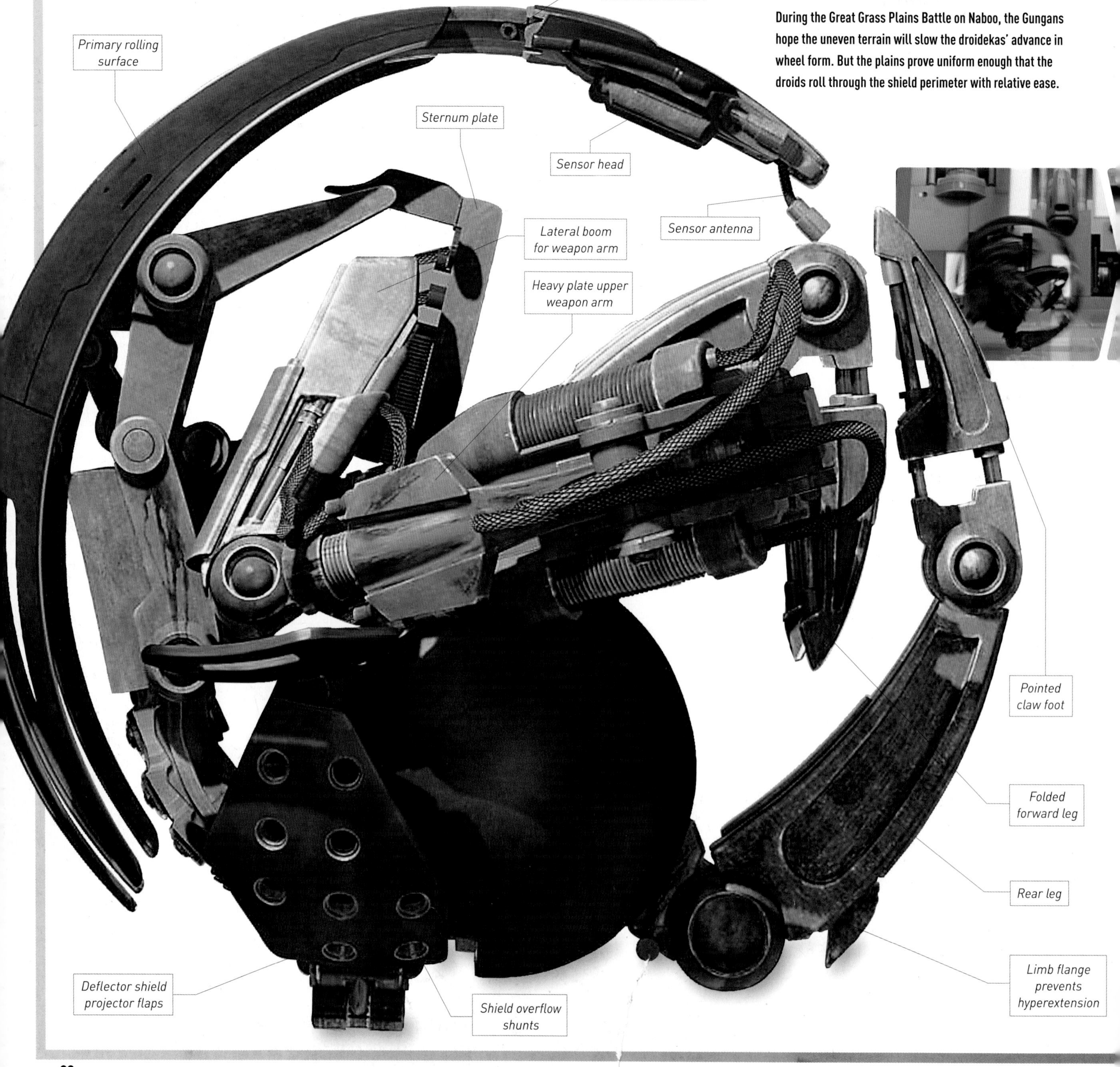

Auxiliary power/ data port

Primary rolling surface

Sternum plate

Sensor head

Lateral boom for weapon arm

Sensor antenna

Heavy plate upper weapon arm

Pointed claw foot

Folded forward leg

Rear leg

Deflector shield projector flaps

Shield overflow shunts

Limb flange prevents hyperextension

Droidekas can roll at high speed, easily running down most fleeing opponents. They have trouble making sharp turns, however, as they topple over easily if they tilt their wheelforms at too steep an angle. Jedi speed is sufficient to outrun them, but few other Trade Federation foes can call upon the Force.

Attack Sequence

Using a combination of momentum and repulsor effects, droidekas unfurl in a matter of seconds from wheel form into a standing position, ready to attack. The dramatic transformation, which recalls the attack pattern of a deadly adult Colicoid, can take unwary opponents by surprise—as the manufacturers intended.

ONE-WAY SHIELD

Droidekas' hazy blue energy shields are polarized, which allows their blaster bolts to pass through the barrier while enemies' return fire dissipates across the spheres of their shields. Secure behind their impenetrable protective globe, droidekas steadily advance on their foes until they are incapacitated.

Experimental models can change shield radius/intensity

Cannons can destroy light vehicles at maximum power

Shield is less powerful at rear

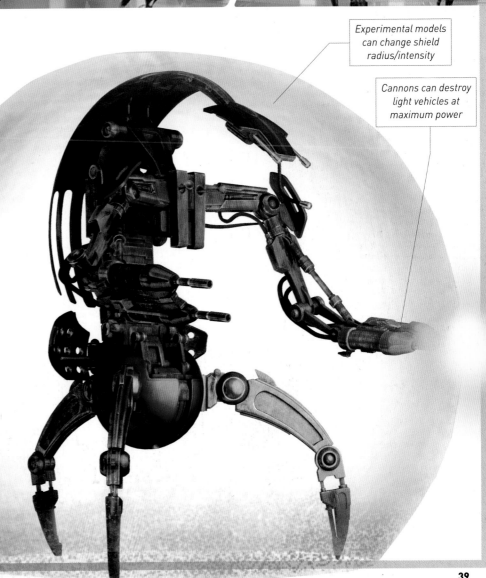

DATA FILE

▶▶ **The Colicoids' price** for supplying the Trade Federation with droidekas and a license to make more was fifty bargeloads of exotic flesh, delivered to their grim homeworld of Colla IV.

▶▶ **The term "droideka"** combines the Basic word "droid" and the suffix "-eka," Colicoid for "drone."

QUEEN AMIDALA

Gold faceframes

Jewel of Zenda

Hair combed over a padded form

A MIDALA RULES AS QUEEN OF THE Naboo at the age of only 14. She was raised in a small mountain village, where her exceptional abilities were recognized early in life. Pushed to develop her capabilities, she became Princess of Theed, the Naboo capital city, at age 12. Amidala was elected Queen upon the abdication of the previous sovereign, Veruna, who became embroiled in outworld politics after a rule of 13 years. The Naboo trusted that Amidala would hold their interests close to her heart—but had no idea of the crisis looming ahead.

Foreknot

Suspensas

Beaded emblems over 240 years old, taken from an earlier queen's gown

Large oversleeves

Painted thumbnail

Black Cyrene silk fabric

Feet hidden for stateliness

AMIDALA'S RESIDENCE GOWN

FOREIGN RESIDENCE GOWN
On Coruscant, Amidala wears a dark gown befitting the gravity of her situation. This subdued foreign residence gown acknowledges Amidala's separation from Naboo and the peril her people face.

Throne-Room Gown

Amidala draws upon Naboo's deeply traditional modes of royal dress and makeup to express the commitment she has to her role. Her extremely formal appearance in the palace throne room helps her project an unwaveringly professional image and warns others not to dismiss her abilities.

Wide shoulders make Amidala seem larger

Shed potolli fur cuffs

White thumbnail polish is the only tradition Amidala retains from her native village

Hand-stitched gold embroidery

Illuminated sein jewel

Amidala sits in state in Theed Palace, hearing cases and reports from the Advisory Council. She has worked well with the Council, though her Head of Security Captain Panaka fears she is ill-prepared for war.

When Queen Amidala travels aboard the Naboo Royal Starship, she holds court in a spacious throne room. Amidala uses a holoprojector to communicate with Governor Sio Bibble back on Naboo.

Wide gown flare hides feet

AMIDALA'S TRAVELING GOWN

Antique tiara

Mauve chersilk hair veil

Full cerlin sleeves

Multi-layered gown

GOLD BEADS

The Queen's gowns are set off with many fine details, such as beads and suspensa ornaments. Many of these come from the palace treasure rooms.

Amidala's stylized white makeup draws upon Naboo's ancient royal customs. The red "scar of remembrance" marks Naboo's time of suffering, before the Great Time of Peace.

NABOO VICTORY PARADE

Golden hairbands

Escoffiate headpiece

Royal Sovereign of Naboo medal

Stylized beauty marks display symmetry

Scar of remembrance divides lip

Minimal jewelry for simplicity

Royal diadem

Jeweled finials

Suspensas made of delicate orichalc finework

Senate Gown

When Amidala pleads for her people before the Galactic Senate, she appears in an extraordinary gown and hairstyle that express the majesty of the free people of Naboo. The regal attire also hides Amidala's feelings and helps her stay courageous and aloof.

Aurate fan in ancient Naboo royal fashion, signifying continuity

Grand finial hairtip ornaments balance escoffiate headpiece

Golden, triple-braided soutache

Petaled cape

Plain white gown expresses the pure happiness of newfound peace

Embossed rosette

Parade Gown

After the victory over the Trade Federation, Amidala appears in a parade gown markedly different from her robes of office. The silken petals of the dress resemble huge, lovely flowers found near Amidala's home village. These flowers bloom only once every 88 years, heralding a time of special celebration.

DATA FILE

▶ **Naboo's monarchy** is not hereditary: rulers are elected by their people on merit. Queen Amidala is not the youngest sovereign ever to rule.

▶ **Amidala can step** down from the throne whenever she chooses.

THE QUEEN'S HANDMAIDENS

Travel Luggage

The special wardrobe containers holding the Queen's wardrobe and jewelry include micrograv devices in their bases. These mechanisms ensure that clothes hang properly even if the closed container is tipped on its side.

DEDICATED AND LOW-KEY, THE ROYAL handmaidens shadow Queen Amidala at all times. This select group maintains Amidala's regal image, assisting behind the scenes with her elaborate gowns, hairstyles, and makeup. They also quietly protect Amidala, acting as secret bodyguards. Upon Amidala's coronation, the handmaidens were hand-picked for their intelligence, courage, fitness, and resemblance to Amidala. Although the Queen has known them for just half a year, she values their company. In particular, she has become close friends with the dependable and cool-headed Sabé.

Feather headdress

Hood to hide face

Gemstone and filigree ear covering

Luggage container

Amidala disguised as a handmaiden

Wardrobe container

TRAVELING IN STYLE
The Royal Starship is equipped with wardrobe containers. From these containers, the handmaidens choose an elaborate dress for the Queen's appearance before the Senate.

Micrograv activates when container is closed

Accessory holders

Climate-controled interior

Rabé

In spite of her young age, Rabé has learned to exercise great patience in her role as handmaiden to the Queen. She soothes Amidala's nerves and helps to prepare her exotic hairstyles, which can require several hours to perfect.

Oversleeves in the Naboo style

Soft trevella cloth

Disguised as Queen Amidala, Sabé is flanked by handmaidens in the throne room of the Royal Starship. The still, expressionless presence of the handmaidens lends dignity to the decoy Queen as she holds court.

Gown tinted with spectra-fade dye

Sabé

The most important handmaiden is Sabé. First in line to become the royal decoy in times of danger, she dresses as the Queen and hides her features with white makeup. Amidala has coached Sabé in regal bearing and speech. Even so, she plays the role with apprehension, concerned that a subtle slip will give her sovereign away.

Battle Dress

In her guise as the Queen, Sabé wears a distinctive battle dress that allows her maximum freedom of movement. In the palace throne room, Sabe's disguise fools the Neimoidian viceroy and allows Amidala to reach a hidden pistol.

Broad waistband

Surcoat

Long skirt made of blast-damping fabric

Eirtaé

Handmaiden Eirtaé comes from a town in a remote river valley. Her family was wealthy and she was taught the demands of etiquette. She helps the other handmaidens—and sometimes the Queen—with royal protocol.

Eirtaé *Yané*

Rabé *Sabé (disguised as Amidala)* *Saché*

IN ATTENDANCE
Just as Amidala wears a particular dress for each different official occasion, the handmaidens dress in matching complementary clothes.

DATA FILE

➡ **Amidala has five** handmaidens: Rabé, Eirtaé, Sabé, Saché, and Yané.

➡ **Rabé, Eirtaé, and Sabé** accompany the Queen when she escapes Theed on the Royal Starship, while Saché and Yané reluctantly stay behind.

Medium-range barrel

Snap-action trigger

ROYAL PISTOL
After being selected, the handmaidens were given bodyguard training. Each is capable of using a pistol to help defend the Queen in the unlikely event of a disturbance or emergency.

Power cell in grip

Shiraya fan headdress worn only by Queen Amidala

Rabé's simple gown sets off the majesty of the Queen's appearance

Wide cowl masks Eirtaé's face

Gown decorated with the Grizmallt symbol

Veda pearl beading

Glass filaments

PADMÉ NABERRIE

Jerba leather cord

Traditional Tatooine sand symbols

Japor ivory wood snippet obtained by Anakin through trading

LUCKY CHARM
Knowing that the future is uncertain, especially his own, Anakin carves a good-luck charm for Padmé. He hopes that she will remember him by this token in spite of what may happen to each of them.

WHENEVER THE QUEEN IS EXPOSED TO DANGER, SHE DISGUISES herself as one of her own handmaidens, taking the name Padmé Naberrie. The identical hooded dresses and similar appearance of Amidala's handmaidens make it easy for Padmé to appear and disappear quietly from the group. When Padmé is among the attendants, handmaiden Sabé impersonates the Queen, subtly taking signals from Padmé regarding royal decisions. Captain Panaka is behind the creation of Amidala's double identity, having explained the old Palace scheme to her upon her coronation. In her guise as Padmé, Amidala accompanies Qui-Gon Jinn to Mos Espa to see for herself what the Jedi is up to.

Simple braids

Rough-spun cloth

Peasant Dress

When Qui-Gon Jinn determines to go into Mos Espa, Padmé decides to keep an eye on him. Captain Panaka, the Naboo Head of Security, promises to look after the ship. Rough peasant clothing helps Padmé blend in as an anonymous farm girl.

In Mos Espa, the disguised Queen finds Qui-Gon Jinn's risky plans not to her liking but she cannot use her regal authority to object. Nonetheless, she realizes that the Jedi Master has the benefit of long experience, and she goes along with his scheme while harboring her doubts.

Glass jewel of little value

Amidala's disguise fools nearly everyone, but nine-year-old Anakin Skywalker quickly sees that Padmé is special. He is drawn to her, and she returns his affection, not quite knowing what to make of the gifted young boy.

Being disguised as Padmé robs Amidala of her regal power, but gives her the freedom to live as a normal person. In Mos Espa, she assists with Anakin's Podracer and helps out where needed.

HANDMAIDEN DISGUISE
Removing her white facepaint is a key element in the success of Amidala's disguise as Padmé. People are so accustomed to the Queen's formal royal appearance that they do not give ordinary-looking Padmé a second glance.

DATA FILE

▶▶ *Padmé and Sabé* practice indirect communication in private, making a game of speaking in cryptic ways. This practice makes it easier for Padmé to guide Sabé's actions as Queen.

▶▶ *As humble Padmé,* Amidala observes things that might not be revealed to the Queen.

Wrist bindings keep out sand and dust

Plain walking boots

Padmé in Battle

Padmé judges that by capturing the Neimoidian leaders she can end the invasion and bring her enemies to justice for their crimes. Her determined presence among her own troops inspires them to succeed against the odds. Sabé remains disguised as the Queen to the end, providing Padmé with a critical advantage at the last minute.

MESSAGE FROM NABOO
While traveling to Coruscant, Padmé is disturbed by the replay of Sio Bibble's hologram transmission, which tells of catastrophic death back on Naboo. Is it a trap? The truth? Or both? It takes great resolve for Padmé to stick to her plan of pleading Naboo's cause in the Galactic Senate when what she most wants is to be with her suffering people.

Hair pulled tightly back for action

High collar conceals blast-absorbing pad

Heavy cloth woven with energy-absorbing fibers to protect against blaster fire

Naboo royal emblem

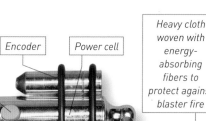

Activator

Encoder

Power cell

Emitter/ sensor tip

SIGNALLING UNIT

Memory cell

Minimal barrel makes blaster easy to hide

Smooth shell design allows blaster to be slipped out from concealment easily

Blaster gas cartridge cap

Snap trigger requires firm squeeze to prevent misfires

Blaster

Padmé and the other handmaidens carry versions of the slim royal pistol. It is designed for practical use and easy concealment. The streamlined blasters pack a mild punch compared to true security guns, but they fire plasma bolts that can be deadly.

SECRET COMMUNICATION
Padmé uses a miniature device to transmit light and data signals silently to Captain Panaka during the battle in Theed.

Energy cell in handgrip

Small, easily concealed blaster

Short-range barrel

RETURN TO THE PALACE
On her return to Naboo, Padmé dons battle dress. In the assault on her own palace, she fights alongside her troops and the Jedi allies in order to reach the throne room and confront the droid invaders. Braving onslaughts of laser bolts, Padmé is quick to return fire without qualms: she knows the battle droids are not living foes.

Calf-length coatskirt protects legs and allows easy movement

In Naboo's most desperate hour, Padmé reveals her secret identity to the Gungan ruler, Boss Nass. She knows that only a clear token of good faith such as this could win over the stubborn Gungan.

High-traction leather tactical boots

Sleeves cut for ease of movement

THE NABOO

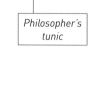

Formal collar

Fashionable Naboo sleeves and cuffs

THE PEOPLE OF NABOO HAVE PROSPERED UNDER THE SECURITY of the Republic, advancing their society without concern for outside threats. Naboo is governed by an elected sovereign, a Governor, and an Advisory Council residing in the Royal Palace at the capital city of Theed. The Naboo live in cities and villages that are thinly scattered on the main landmass of their planet. A love of art is deeply seated in Naboo culture, taking such forms as grand architecture and elaborate clothing fashions. The Naboo regard their refined way of life as a birthright, but they will find that it is a luxury that they will have to defend.

The planet Naboo is small, green, and honeycombed by a curious crustal substructure that is riddled with cave passages.

Sio Bibble

As governor of Naboo, the outspoken Sio Bibble oversees all matters brought to the Queen's attention. He also chairs the Advisory Council, and deals directly with regional representatives and town governing officials in day-to-day administration.

CULTURAL CAPITAL
In addition to the Royal Palace, the greatest Naboo libraries, museums, shrines, theaters, and conservatories are located in Theed. The city's buildings are designed in the classical Naboo style.

Sio Bibble is loath to concede to Captain Panaka's dire warnings of greater need for armament. A noble philosopher, he even refuses to change his mind during his planet's most desperate hour.

FUNERAL TEMPLE
The Naboo believe that cremation returns the life force of the dead to the planet. Bodies are burned on a pyre in the temple, with the ashes then dropped from the Livet Bridge into the River Solleu below.

Philosopher's tunic

Governor's boots

Theed

The crown jewel of Naboo civilization is the city of Theed, built at the edge of a great plateau where the River Solleu winds its way toward a spectacular waterfall. Artisans, architects, and urban planners are all valued highly in Naboo culture, and their splendid city is a special testament to their efforts.

THEED PALACE

Built centuries ago, the Royal Palace is the largest building in Theed. Its courts are used for meetings, dinners, parties, cultural events, and visiting dignitaries. The palace blends historic design facets with automatic doors, communications systems, and area-specific climate control.

Amidala seated before her Advisory Council

Columns made of polished Naboo stone

Large windows lend serenity

Palace Guard

Holoprojector retracts when not in use

CORUSCANT CALL
Elegant circles of polished marble hide a holoprojector set in the throne room's floor.

THE ADVISORY COUNCIL

The members of the Royal Advisory Council present matters to the Queen and offer her their expertise. The Council frequently changes the composition of its membership, bringing a range of scholars, artists, and interested community members into the Queen's audience.

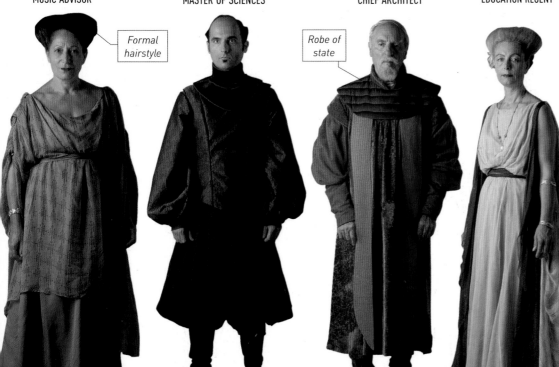

HELA BRANDES
MUSIC ADVISOR

Formal hairstyle

GRAF ZAPALO
MASTER OF SCIENCES

HUGO ECKENER
CHIEF ARCHITECT

Robe of state

LUFTA SHIF
EDUCATION REGENT

ROYAL GATEWAY

The palace's frontcourt is watched over by six statues of winged warriors representing strength, honor, fidelity, steadfastness, wisdom, and charity. The Six Virtues were sculpted by the legendary Fasano Eckener 500 years ago.

DATA FILE

➡ **The bulbous shaak** creature is native to Naboo and prized for its meat.

NABOO JEWELRY

Zoorif feather motif

Organic chif stone

FORMAL FUTHARK

The Naboo alphabet has a traditional handwritten form, the futhork, and a formal form, called the futhark. The formal script, based on ovals, is used for purposes such as spacecraft identifications and control labels.

SOCIAL FABRIC

Clothing is often used as a form of social communication. During the Trade Federation blockade, citizens of Theed make subtle use of Naboo color and fashion symbolism to express their support or opposition to the Queen's policies.

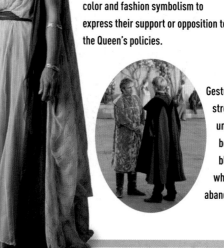

Gestures of reassurance in the streets of Theed mask underlying tensions as people begin to grow hungry from the blockade. Some wonder whether their Queen will abandon them for her own safety.

CAPTAIN PANAKA

High officer headgear

Naboo Security crest

AS HEAD OF SECURITY FOR QUEEN AMIDALA, CAPTAIN
Panaka oversees every branch of the volunteer Royal Naboo Security Forces
and is personally responsible for the Queen's safety. Panaka was appointed after
his predecessor, Captain Magneta, failed to prevent the death of the former King
Veruna, who had gone into hiding upon his abdication. Veruna's "accidental" death
was covered up—even from the Queen—and Magneta quietly resigned. Panaka
sees the increasingly dangerous state of affairs in the galaxy and argues for
stronger security measures to protect the Queen and Naboo itself. Despite
this, the Advisory Council convinces Amidala to act in accordance with Naboo's
traditional pacifism. Panaka doubts this noble policy will succeed, but it takes
the terror of an invasion to bring his point home.

Comlink in holster

Leather jerkin covers thin anti-blast armor plates

Panaka has the confidence
of an experienced man and
relies on his own judgment
even when Jedi Knights
step in. He believes that
Qui-Gon Jinn's actions risk
the Queen's safety and the
fate of Naboo.

Comlink attachment

Belt clip bracket

Sturdy casing

COMLINK HOLDER

Rangefinding scope

Grappling hook (far side)

Primary sighting scope

Blaster gas cell chamber

Heat radiator ridges

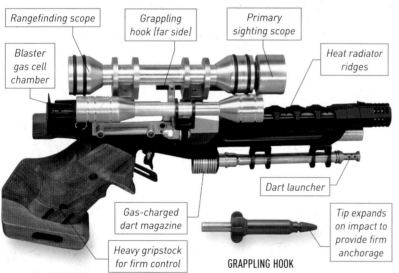

Dart launcher

Gas-charged dart magazine

Heavy gripstock for firm control

Tip expands on impact to provide firm anchorage

GRAPPLING HOOK

Voice pickup

Transmitter

Handgrip

Panaka's security forces use small ground craft like the Gian
landspeeder for patrols and general operations. These light
speeders are some of the few assets Panaka has in his effort to
retake Theed Palace from the invading droids.

Blaster

The Royal Palace Guard use multi-function Security S-5 blaster guns. Not only
do these weapons fire deadly blaster bolts, harmless sting charges, and
anaesthetic microdarts, the S-5 blaster even includes a liquid-cable shooter that
can coil around an enemy or let soldiers scale walls via a grappling-hook tip.

COMLINK
Captain Panaka uses a
master security comlink
to keep in touch with
his volunteer divisions,
employing separate
channels for
command clarity.

DATA FILE

▶▶ **Captain Panaka gained** combat experience in a
Republic Special Task Force fighting against space
pirates in the sector containing
the Naboo system.

▶▶ **The Naboo Royal** Security
Forces include the Security Guard,
Palace Guard, and Space Fighter
Corps. Local police answer to
civilian authorities, not to Panaka.

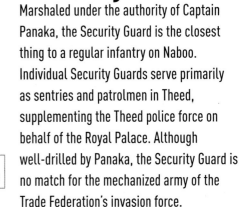

Facing the Trade Federation forces, Panaka and his Palace Guard fight with determined efficiency to return the Queen to the throne.

Security Officer

Panaka's few top officers are loyal but mostly unfamiliar with real danger. During the Trade Federation invasion, they work hard to maintain order on Naboo.

Security Guard

Marshaled under the authority of Captain Panaka, the Security Guard is the closest thing to a regular infantry on Naboo. Individual Security Guards serve primarily as sentries and patrolmen in Theed, supplementing the Theed police force on behalf of the Royal Palace. Although well-drilled by Panaka, the Security Guard is no match for the mechanized army of the Trade Federation's invasion force.

Palace Guard

The Palace Guard is the highly trained bodyguard of the Queen and court. While the Security Guard functions as a militia, the Palace Guard is made up of dedicated soldiers who typically experience battle off-planet and return to protect the Queen out of loyalty. Although few in number, the Palace Guard is the backbone of Naboo security.

Officer's headgear

Officer's pistol

Naboo Security crest

Wrist guard

CR-2 basic blaster, built to last

Resilient armor plates

Combat helmet

Liquid cable shooter

Chin strap

Unarmored joints for agility

Utility belt

Leather jerkin

Utility belt

Blast-damping armor

No leg armor for mobility

Traditional full cut thigh

Studded forearm plate for hand-to-hand combat

Shin protectors buckle over short boots

Auxiliary gear straps

High-traction, quiet-soled security boots

Uniform color denotes Security Guard

SPACE FIGHTER CORPS

THE PILOTS OF THE NABOO SPACE FIGHTER CORPS PATROL space around the planet and serve as Queen Amidala's honorguard while she is offworld. As Naboo is a largely peaceful world, the all-volunteer corps of pilots must turn elsewhere for combat experience, winning their wings protecting merchant convoys, in service as mercenaries, or flying as privateers for distant star systems. While other systems' pilots are more battle-hardened, the Naboo corps is quite capable, excelling at formation tactics honed in hours of drills with their custom-built Naboo N-1 starfighters. That preparation serves them well against the droid starfighters of the Trade Federation.

FLYING HELMET

Welded joints of armor shell

Flying goggles

Automatic distress beacon

Anti-glare brim

Built-in communicator system

Flying jacket

N-1 Starfighter

Partly finished in gleaming chromium to indicate royal status, N-1 starfighters sport radial engines of Nubian make in a J-configuration spaceframe. Assisted by an astromech droid, starfighters are fast and agile, but prone to uncontrollable spins when the engines suffer damage.

Heat sink finial

Cockpit

Astromech loads into fighter from below

Pilot safety harness attaches to ship's seat

N-1 FIGHTER

Power charge collector plugs into hangar systems

Bright colors typical of Naboo style

Power diversion display

Power delivery gauges

Reference horizon

Celestial hemisphere

Flying gloves

DATA FILE

➤ **Naboo pilots must** gain experience flying utility craft before they are permitted to take the controls of a coveted N-1 starfighter.

➤ **Only a few** lucky pilots have ever flown royal escort duty all the way to Coruscant, most never having left Naboo's sector.

Orientation grids

SYSTEMS MONITOR

NAVIGATION SCAN

Space Fighter Corps overcoat

N-1 STARFIGHTER READOUTS
Starfighter pilots constantly monitor navigation and systems information from readout panels arrayed in the cockpit.

Trade Federation droid starfighters

Naboo pilot-issue boots

TACTICAL SCOPE

ROYAL PERFECTION
The Royal Starship is quite unlike craft from other planets. Its distinctive interior is characterized by elegant curves and a clean, refined look. As with much Naboo design, utility is secondary to aesthetic concerns.

Hand-finished chromium is a royal prerogative

Starship carries no weapons

Throne room

Heat sink finial makes fuel burn cleaner

Sublight engine

Royal Starship

The gleaming Naboo Royal Starship conveys Queen Amidala to formal state appearances in matchless style. Built on Naboo using foreign-made engine and technology components, the ship blends the Naboo love of art with the industrial power available from other worlds.

Ric Olié

The top pilot in the Space Fighter Corps is Ric Olié, a veteran flier who answers directly to Captain Panaka. Perfectly capable of flying any craft on Naboo, it is Ric Olié's honor to captain the Queen's Royal Starship. The run through the Trade Federation blockade taxes Olié's flying abilities to the limit, and even he doubts whether they can get through alive.

High-resolution eyepiece

Talo-effect "lens" allows subatomic analysis

MESON TALOSCOPE

Enlarged section showing damage

Power cells pulse energy through equipment to be tested

DAMAGE MONITORS
The Royal Starship has elaborate built-in systems to monitor equipment. When the ship suffers laser hits from the Trade Federation blockade, pilot Ric Olié can see at a glance exactly what has been damaged.

Starship overview

ENGINEERING ANALYSIS BOARD

Diagnostic block

HIGH-END INSTRUMENTS
High-precision diagnostic and analysis instruments onboard the Royal Starship allow the crew to conduct a variety of tests. The wide range of instruments is capable of anticipating problems before they occur.

Hyperdrive diagnostic monitor

Warning mark indicates energy leak

View mode indicator allows different internal representations

Touch control

Area of field leakage

Naboo-made charge planes

Damaged priming pylons

Hyperdrive Core

A dazzling example of Naboo style, the hyperdrive core of the Royal Starship is an intricate maze of charge planes and effect channels that allows the ship to slip smoothly beyond lightspeed. When the Nubian-made hyperdrive generator inside the core fails under the energy overloads encountered in battle, the Naboo begin to learn the realities of their dependence on the outside world.

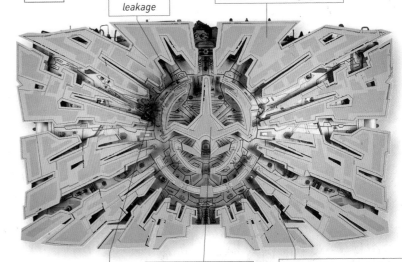

Overload burnout scar

Core chamber holds Nubian T-14 generator

Hyperdrive effect channels improve supralight performance

THEED HANGAR

FOR NABOO'S SPACE PILOTS, THE HANGAR IN THEED'S
Royal Palace is home: It's where they practice maneuvers in flight simulators, where they work with astromech droids to maintain their craft, and where they lounge around swapping stories about derring-do behind the stick. Though Naboo is a peaceful world, the hangar always hums with activity, as pilots, technicians, and flight controllers rub shoulders with royal visitors. During the Invasion of Naboo, however, Theed Hangar becomes the epicenter of an uprising, witnessing more action than ever before.

FULL-THROTTLE EXIT

The Theed Hangar sits some 50 meters from the edge of cliffs shrouded in greenery, near a vertiginous waterfall at the end of the River Solleu known as the Virdugo Plunge. With the cliffs so close, this is no place for timid pilots. When the Trade Federation invades Naboo, the Royal Starship launches from Theed Hangar, carrying Naboo's Queen in a daring bid for freedom.

Enter the Hangar

The N-1 starfighter was developed exclusively for Naboo's royal security forces. The fighter combines standard internal components with a custom spaceframe. Its sleek lines and chromium finish make it beautiful; twin cannons and proton torpedoes make it deadly. Fighters ready for launch are kept connected to the palace power grid through plug-in sockets on their long, graceful tails, and bob gently in the air on their repulsorlifts.

- N-1 starfighter plugged into hangar power grid
- Landing lights
- Pristine marble deck flooring
- Vacuum unit
- Droid loader

HANGAR LADDER

When a launch order comes, astromechs load through hatches in the bottoms of the fighters, while pilots scurry up ladders kept at the ready. Qui-Gon orders Anakin to hide in an N-1 starfighter during the Battle for Naboo.

Vital Equipment

The main flight deck of Theed Hangar is filled with astromechs and droids of all shapes and sizes going about their mechanical business, as well as specialist flight equipment to help ease the workload of the Theed Hangar ground crew and pilots.

SCRUBBER DROIDS

Scrubber droids are common sights in hangars, where they constantly sniff for spilled fuel and other volatile substances, vacuum spills into their insulated storage tanks, and move swiftly to extinguish fires before they can spread and threaten the lives of organic crews.

- Antenna for communication with Theed Palace computer system
- Non-slip treads
- Stereo sniffers find drops of dangerous leaked fuel
- Monocular navigation photoreceptor
- Primitive droid brain positions ladder at proper fighter
- Fuel scrubbers (on underside)

Theed Ground Crew

Dressed in eye-catching yellow jump suits, Theed hangar's ground crew assists pilots and astromechs in ensuring that craft are in top condition and ready to fly at a moment's notice. Crewers are trained in everything from flight operations to starship maintenance, and can perform any number of tasks if called upon.

PANAKA'S PLAN

After Amidala returns to Naboo, Captain Panaka contacts underground resistance fighters in Theed. They infiltrate the hangar and verify that the N-1 starfighters are still operational. Panaka's agents then break into the computer system and upload plans for the raid on the Droid Control Ship.

The Trade Federation held the hangar's mechanics and other staff captive on site so they could handle Neimoidian vessels once a treaty made their occupation legitimate. Freed, they rush to strike back against their captors.

> Blast helmet includes sound-dampening layers

> Tool pouch holds various gadgets

> Coolant valve and vent complex

DATA FILE

➺ **The hangar floor** is studded with coolant reservoirs and guidance beacons that can be retracted below the deck.

➺ **The Royal Starship** normally sits in the middle of the hangar and can be prepped for takeoff in just minutes.

> Extensible power feed with rotating connectors

POWER DROID

Veril Line Systems' GZ-5 energy units are essentially mobile batteries that provide energy when a power grid is offline, overtaxed, or out of reach.

> Sensor suite for vacuum unit

DROID LOADER

Astromechs' wheeled legs and rocket boosters enable them to get around adeptly, but in situations where droids need to be transported in groups or while shut down, droid loaders come into use.

> Extensible platform

> Driver's station

VACUUM UNIT

Industrial Automaton's wheeled S-X Vac-u-Bot specializes in draining fuel and coolant from ships, and probing and fixing lines and reservoirs for clogs. Vac-u-Bots and scrubber droids sometimes get in each other's way and quarrel until given new orders by a supervisor droid.

> THEED GROUD CREW MEMBER BERNIE JABESQ

> Heavy boots protect against heat and corrosive fuel

R2-D2

A UTILITY DROID WITH A MIND OF HIS OWN, THERE IS MORE to R2-D2 than his ordinary appearance would suggest. Just one of several droids assigned to the Naboo Royal Starship, R2-D2 replaces blown fuses, installs new wiring, polishes floors, and does whatever else is necessary to maintain the gleaming vessel in perfect working condition. For a utility droid, R2-D2 is equipped with remarkable tenacity and drive to accomplish his missions. Such dedication would ordinarily go unnoticed, but when crisis envelops the Royal Starship, R2-D2 becomes a hero.

LUBRICATING ARM
R2 uses this arm to service starfighters and other machinery, heating, pressurizing, and spraying lubricant deep within an engine or other machinery.

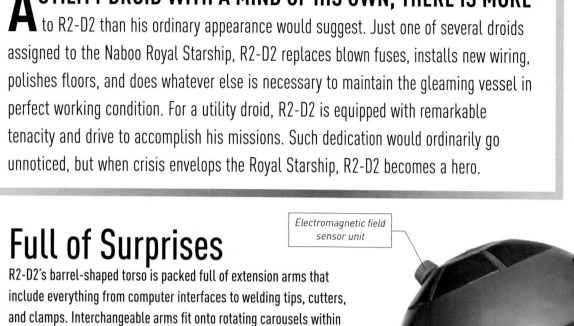

Lubricant filter

Adjustable spray nozzle

SCANNER ANTENNA
Housed within his dome, R2's antenna allows him to scan for a wide range of signals, from audio transmissions to the electromagnetic patterns produced by living things.

Signal amplifier

Full of Surprises

R2-D2's barrel-shaped torso is packed full of extension arms that include everything from computer interfaces to welding tips, cutters, and clamps. Interchangeable arms fit onto rotating carousels within R2's body, which allows him to quickly select the proper arm for the job and deploy it to assist his friends.

Information buffer

COMPUTER INTERFACE ARM
R2 uses this arm to communicate with a variety of computer systems, entering commands, downloading information, or uploading programs.

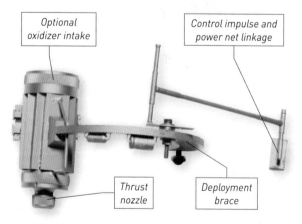

Optional oxidizer intake

Control impulse and power net linkage

Thrust nozzle

Deployment brace

ROCKET THRUSTER
Accessory rocket thrusters give R2 units the ability to propel themselves through air or space.

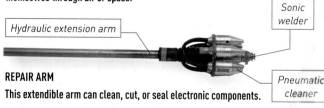

Hydraulic extension arm

Sonic welder

REPAIR ARM
This extendible arm can clean, cut, or seal electronic components.

Pneumatic cleaner

Electromagnetic field sensor unit

Primary photoreceptor and radar eye

Inference pulse stabilizers

Luminescent diagnostic display

Hydraulic arm shaft

Heat exhaust

Sand-proof joints

Extendible third leg

All-terrain main drive tread

Powerbus cables

Swivel-mounted tread

In-Flight Repairs

Astromech droids commonly carry out a wide variety of mechanical repairs and information-retrieval tasks, and are little noticed in spaceports and aboard ships. R2's tenacity in repairing the Naboo Royal Starship wins him the gratitude of the ship's crew. They know the little droid has saved their lives.

Only a droid can repair the Naboo Royal Starship's damaged shield generator: The work is much too delicate for an organic being to perform quickly, even without the danger of laserfire. The crew can only watch anxiously as R2 goes about his work.

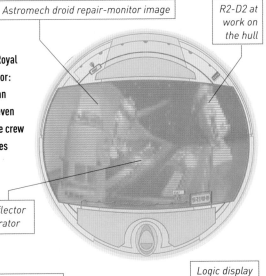

Astromech droid repair-monitor image

R2-D2 at work on the hull

Damaged deflector shield generator

Serving the Queen

Amidala's Royal Starship carries a complement of six astromech droids: R2-D2, R2-N3, G8-R3, R2-B1, R2-R9, and R2-M5. Droids R2-B1, G8-R3, and R2-R9 are all destroyed while trying to repair the ship's damaged shield generator, while R2-N3 and R2-M5 are blasted off the hull while fixing an imbalance in the starboard engines.

Dome sensor hatch

Holographic projector

R2-B1

Data card input

Logic display function

R2-M5

Recharge coupling

Polarity sink

R2-R9

DROID HOLD

In a small chamber on the lowest deck of the Naboo Royal Starship, R2-D2 recharges between work projects and waits with other astromech droids for assignments. A repulsorlift tube at one end of the hold conveys the droids to the outside of the ship for work on the hull during flight.

CO-PILOT

Standard astromech droids are used in many space fighters as onboard flight support. They slot into sockets behind the cockpit, plugging into all systems and effectively co-piloting the space fighter. R2-D2 accompanies Anakin Skywalker into battle over the skies of Naboo in the droid socket of a Naboo N-1 Starfighter.

DATA FILE

➤ **R2-D2 is owned** by the Royal House of Naboo. He was assigned to the Queen's ship because of his outstanding performance record.

➤ **Artoo's head can** telescope up so that he can see out of the tight neck of a Naboo starfighter droid socket.

JAR JAR BINKS

AN AMPHIBIOUS GUNGAN NATIVE TO NABOO, JAR JAR IS A

luckless exile from his home city, Otoh Gunga. He now lives in the swamps, where he survives on his own, eating raw shellfish and other such swamp fare. His long muscular tongue helps him to scoop mollusks out of their shells and tasty gumbols out of their tree burrows. During the invasion of Naboo, Qui-Gon Jinn runs into and rescues Jar Jar. The simple Gungan's sense of honor binds him to Qui-Gon for life, even though the Jedi would much rather do without him at first.

At first, Obi-Wan Kenobi dismisses Jar Jar as an inconvenient life form to have around. However, the Gungan quickly proves useful by telling the Jedi of an underwater city where they can escape from the ground forces of the Trade Federation.

Gungan Survivor

Like all Gungans, Jar Jar's skeleton is made of cartilage, making him flexible and rubbery. Even his skull and jaws are elastic, giving the simple Gungan a wide range of facial expressions. Jar Jar's character, like his body, is resilient and able to bend to changes of fortune without letting his spirit break. Whether alone, in the company of Jedi, or even among royalty, Jar Jar blunders through life with light-hearted good humor in spite of his occasional panic attacks.

GUNGAN HANDCUFFS

Nictitating membrane

Nostrils seal underwater

Large teeth for cracking shellfish

Four-fingered hand

Cartilaginous skeleton is stiff but not brittle

Partially retractable eyestalk

Tough skin near head for burrowing

Haillu (earlobes) for display

Tight vocal cords produce high-pitched voice

Lanky build from life in exile

Mottled skin for camouflage

Fashion statement

When Qui-Gon Jinn goes to Mos Espa in search of hyperdrive parts, Jar Jar accompanies him. Qui-Gon knows that this odd Gungan will help him blend into the diverse population of strange life forms inhabiting the city. Meanwhile, Jar Jar worries about exposing his amphibian skin to the heat and suns.

JAR JAR'S EXILE

Jar Jar is reticent about the reason for his exile from Otoh Gunga, glossing over the fact that he accidentally flooded most of Boss Nass's mansion and several adjoining bubbles while working as a waiter at a party. As this was not Jar Jar's first serious accident, Boss Nass was furious, and Jar Jar was exiled from his own city under pain of death.

Jar Jar is well known to the city patrol of Otoh Gunga, which has extricated him from all kinds of trouble in the past—from petty squabbles over food theft to the commotion Jar Jar caused when he inadvertently opened half of the Otoh Gunga Zoo bubbles. They know Boss Nass will not be pleased to see the infamous Gungan in his chambers again.

General Jar Jar

Boss Nass misinterprets Jar Jar's connections with the newly-favored Naboo royalty as maturity and makes him a general in the Gungan Grand Army—much to the dismay of the troops he is to "command." Jar Jar lives up to their expectations when he panics during combat, falls off his mount, and instantly surrenders when surrounded. Fortunately, few soldiers pay the new general any attention and, since the Gungans win the battle anyway, Boss Nass is none the wiser.

Cesta

Determined warrior stance

Tough, stubby feet

Castoff stretchy Gungan pants

Spongy kneecaps

Powerful calf muscles for swimming

Tight trouser ends keep out swamp crawlies

DATA FILE

➤ **Jar Jar's insatiable** curiosity frequently lands him in trouble. He comes close to learning a permanent lesson when he catches his tongue in Anakin's Podracer engine binders.

➤ **Jar Jar speaks a** pidgin Gungan dialect of Galactic Basic. Few Gungans speak the pure Gungan language.

Gungan Sub

Panicky Jar Jar is possibly the worst navigator the Jedi could have as they make their way through the underwater passages that connect Otoh Gunga to the Naboo capital city, Theed. He has paid no attention to submarine piloting or to finding his way beyond his swamp home. To make matters worse, Jar Jar is petrified of deep-sea creatures lurking in the caverns.

Mollusk and gumbol breakfast

Starboard cargo bubble

Organic Gungan design

Cockpit hydrostatic bubble

Electromotive drive fins

When hungry, Jar Jar eats nearly anything without a second thought, a habit learned from being exiled in the Naboo swamps. In Mos Espa market, he tries to steal a bite from a street vendor hoping that his long tongue will make short work of the morsel.

THE GUNGANS

GUNGANS EVOLVED IN THE SWAMPS OF NABOO, BECOMING almost equally well adapted to life on land and in water. These amphibious beings live in underwater cities hidden in deep lakes, breathing air or water with their compound lungs. Gungans trade with the Naboo for certain items of technology, but manufacture everything else they need from the resources of their underwater habitat. Although Gungans use mechanized vehicles, they have a close affinity with the natural world and prefer to utilize living mounts and beasts of burden when going about their daily lives.

Rep hood

Otoh swirls

Rep robe

Rep Teers

Rep Teers is responsible for the power supply that sustains the hydrostatic bubbles of Otoh Gunga. He is part of the Gungan Rep Council: a group of appointed officers who are responsible for various areas of government and assist Boss Nass in important decisions. The officers' special clothing indicates the dignity of their office.

Older Gungans have hair-like finlets

Whiskers indicate maturity

Captain Tarpals

Kaadu patrol chief in Otoh Gunga, Captain Tarpals is usually on the lookout for thieves or dangerous water creatures that might threaten the Gungan populace. To the weary Tarpals, accident-prone Jar Jar Binks is a familiar menace who occupies his own special category.

Rep Lyonie   Rep Slarm   Boss Nass   Rep Teers   Rep Been

THE BOARD ROOM
Headed by Boss Nass, the Rep Council meets in a prestigious new boardroom connected to a suite of offices and reached via 14 elaborate foyer bubbles. The contrast between this grand setting and the workaday business of the Council causes much amusement in Otoh Gunga.

Boss Nass

Ruler of Otoh Gunga, the largest lake city, Boss Nass is a stern, old-fashioned Gungan who speaks Galactic Basic with a strong accent. He commands great authority even in communities beyond Otoh Gunga and has grown large and prosperous in his advancing years. It is in Boss Nass's power alone to summon the Gungan Grand Army, which is made up of Gungans from all settlements.

Mangana aqua jewel

Crown of rulership

Prosperous face

Epaulets of military authority

Swirl designs typical of Otoh Gungan clothing

Four-fingered hand

Long coat denotes social importance

Golden coat clasp

Gungan sandals

A fair but stubborn ruler, Boss Nass resents the arrogance of the Naboo, who regard Gungans as primitive simply because they do not embrace a technological lifestyle. He finds it best all round to minimize contact with humans.

Like all the Naboo, Queen Amidala was taught to think of Gungans as barbarians. But when the planet is faced with invasion, she realizes that her people and the Gungans must work together or die. Humbly finding the courage to ask Boss Nass for help, Amidala forges a new friendship between the two cultures. Deeply impressed with her gesture, Boss Nass changes his views as well.

DATA FILE

➤➤ **Boss Nass has** the distinctive green skin and hooded eyes of the old Ankura lineage that hails from an isolated swamp village. His distant ancestors united with the Otolla Gungans who founded Otoh Gunga.

➤➤ **The Globe of Peace** is blown glass encasing locap plasma.

Rep Been

A keeper of ancient Gungan records, Rep Been knows the secrets of old Gungan hiding places. As Boss Nass's strongest ally on the Council, Been supported the Otoh Gunga governor's decision to evacuate the city after the Trade Federation attacked, and helped organize the retreat to the Sacred Place.

Contemplative pose

GUNGAN NABOO

LOCATED FAR FROM CONTACT WITH THE NABOO, THE GUNGANS' underwater cities glisten like scintillating jewelry. The Gungan capital city, Otoh Gunga, prides itself on being independent of foreign influences. Nonetheless, Otoh Gunga relies upon a quiet but vital trade with the Naboo. In this, as in the danger they face from the Trade Federation's invading armies, the Gungans find that they are more connected with outsiders than they would like to believe. If they are to continue to live in peace, the Gungans will have to overcome their isolationist tendencies, allying with the Naboo to expel the invaders of their common home.

Otoh Gunga

The magical gleam of Otoh Gunga is hidden in the deep waters of Lake Paonga. Powerful hydrostatic membrane fields keep water out of the dwelling bubbles and give the city its characteristic jewel-like look. The various-sized bubbles are anchored to the lake's floor with huge stone pillars.

Hydrostatic bubbles of Otoh Gunga

PAONGA'S SECRET
Nearly a million Gungans dwell in Otoh Gunga. The city's heart is a dense cluster of bubbles that house its public spaces, including the storied Ancient Quarter. The central city is ringed by the Otoh Villages, beyond which are satellite clusters, some cast out from other cities.

GUNGAN DESIGNS
The undersea world's forms are a strong influence on Gungan aesthetics: Gungan artists love the spheres of air bubbles and eggs, the curves of leaves and fishes, and the spikes and fans of aquatic grasses.

Typical Gungan design

Atmospheric purifiers

Kernode assembly for larger bubbles

Generators

Hydrostatic field

Utanode

Counterphase harmonizing struts

Utanode assembly brace

Portal zone

Habitation floor

Field focusing element

Hydrostatic field generators

GUNGAN SACRED PLACE

The Gungan Sacred Place lies in the foothills of the Gallo Mountains. Here, the woodlands are dotted with tumbled statues and derelict temples, the work of the Naboo Elders. The Elders have been extinct for millennia, and peko-pekos now nest in the ruins they left behind, filling the air with raucous calls.

Stabilizer

Ancient Refuge

When trouble comes, Gungans retreat into the swamps of Naboo, following nearly invisible paths they have used for generations. In the swamplands, they are surrounded by the birds and beasts of primordial Naboo, and draw strength from the richness and vitality of life on their homeworld.

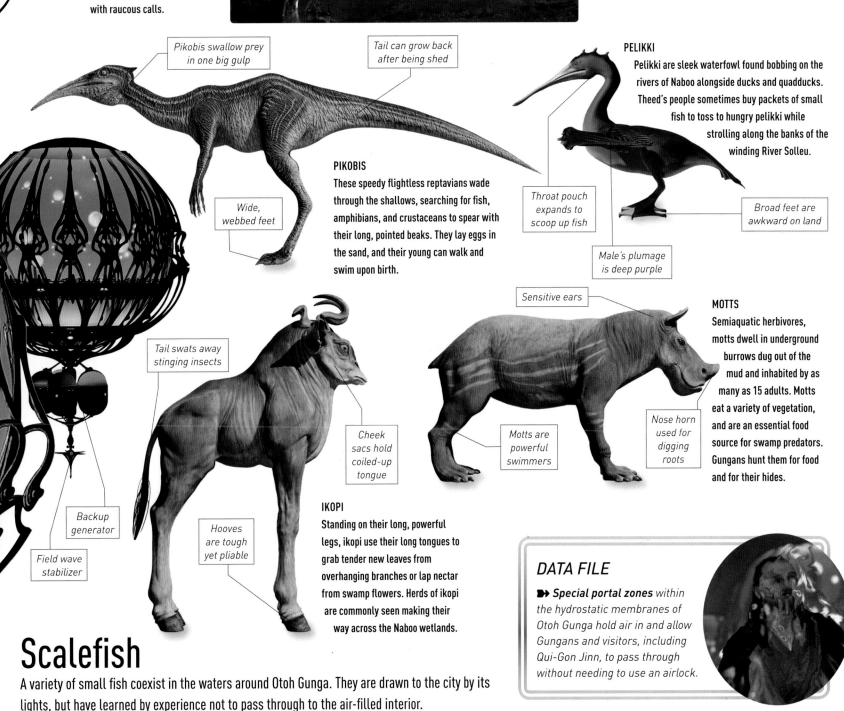

Pikobis swallow prey in one big gulp

Tail can grow back after being shed

PELIKKI

Pelikki are sleek waterfowl found bobbing on the rivers of Naboo alongside ducks and quadducks. Theed's people sometimes buy packets of small fish to toss to hungry pelikki while strolling along the banks of the winding River Solleu.

PIKOBIS

These speedy flightless reptavians wade through the shallows, searching for fish, amphibians, and crustaceans to spear with their long, pointed beaks. They lay eggs in the sand, and their young can walk and swim upon birth.

Wide, webbed feet

Throat pouch expands to scoop up fish

Broad feet are awkward on land

Male's plumage is deep purple

Sensitive ears

MOTTS

Semiaquatic herbivores, motts dwell in underground burrows dug out of the mud and inhabited by as many as 15 adults. Motts eat a variety of vegetation, and are an essential food source for swamp predators. Gungans hunt them for food and for their hides.

Tail swats away stinging insects

Cheek sacs hold coiled-up tongue

Motts are powerful swimmers

Nose horn used for digging roots

Backup generator

Field wave stabilizer

Hooves are tough yet pliable

IKOPI

Standing on their long, powerful legs, ikopi use their long tongues to grab tender new leaves from overhanging branches or lap nectar from swamp flowers. Herds of ikopi are commonly seen making their way across the Naboo wetlands.

Scalefish

A variety of small fish coexist in the waters around Otoh Gunga. They are drawn to the city by its lights, but have learned by experience not to pass through to the air-filled interior.

DATA FILE

➤ **Special portal zones** within the hydrostatic membranes of Otoh Gunga hold air in and allow Gungans and visitors, including Qui-Gon Jinn, to pass through without needing to use an airlock.

MEE

Poison spine

FAA

RAY

TEE

SEE

LAA

GUNGAN WARFARE

LONG UNITED BY TREATIES, THE GUNGANS do not fight the Naboo or each other. Many years ago they drove off the last invaders to threaten them. Nonetheless they maintain an armed force for tradition and defense against attack by sea monsters. The Grand Army employs both technological wizardry and traditional weaponry. Its primary focus is on defense, for which animal-mounted shield generators are used. For attack, the Gungans hurl plasmic energy balls. Soldiers of the Grand Army are inexperienced, but their resolve comes from a firm sense of duty and justice.

War Tools

Gungan ammunition consists of a strange form of highly destructive plasmic energy that bursts upon impact. These energy balls are prepared in different sizes and are hurled into the air by a variety of long and short range throwing sticks, simple catapults... and occasionally by accident.

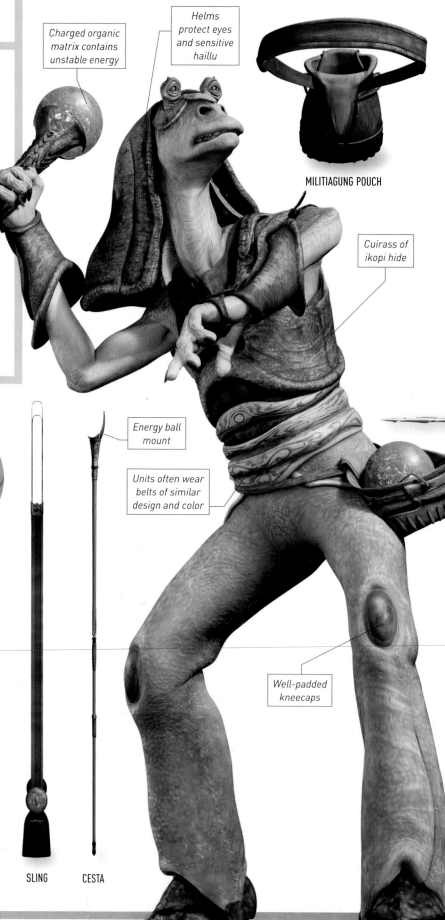

Charged organic matrix contains unstable energy

Helms protect eyes and sensitive haillu

MILITIAGUNG POUCH

Cuirass of ikopi hide

Energy ball mount

Units often wear belts of similar design and color

Well-padded kneecaps

Emerging from the swamps, Gungan troops from all the underwater communities unite by stages into the single body of the Grand Army. Gungan soldiers know that they must face the Trade Federation army to ensure their people's survival and freedom.

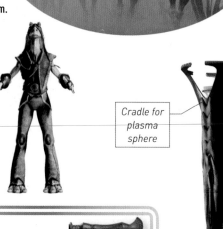

CAVALRY

The Grand Army consists mostly of militiagungs, or part-time soldiers. Individuals provide their own uniforms, resulting in some variation in gear and clothing.

Cradle for plasma sphere

DATA FILE

➻ **To be effective,** militiagungs take orders from professional soldiers assigned as their commanders.

➻ **Every militiagung practices** identifying horn, drum, and whistle signals at long distances.

ATLATL   SLING   CESTA

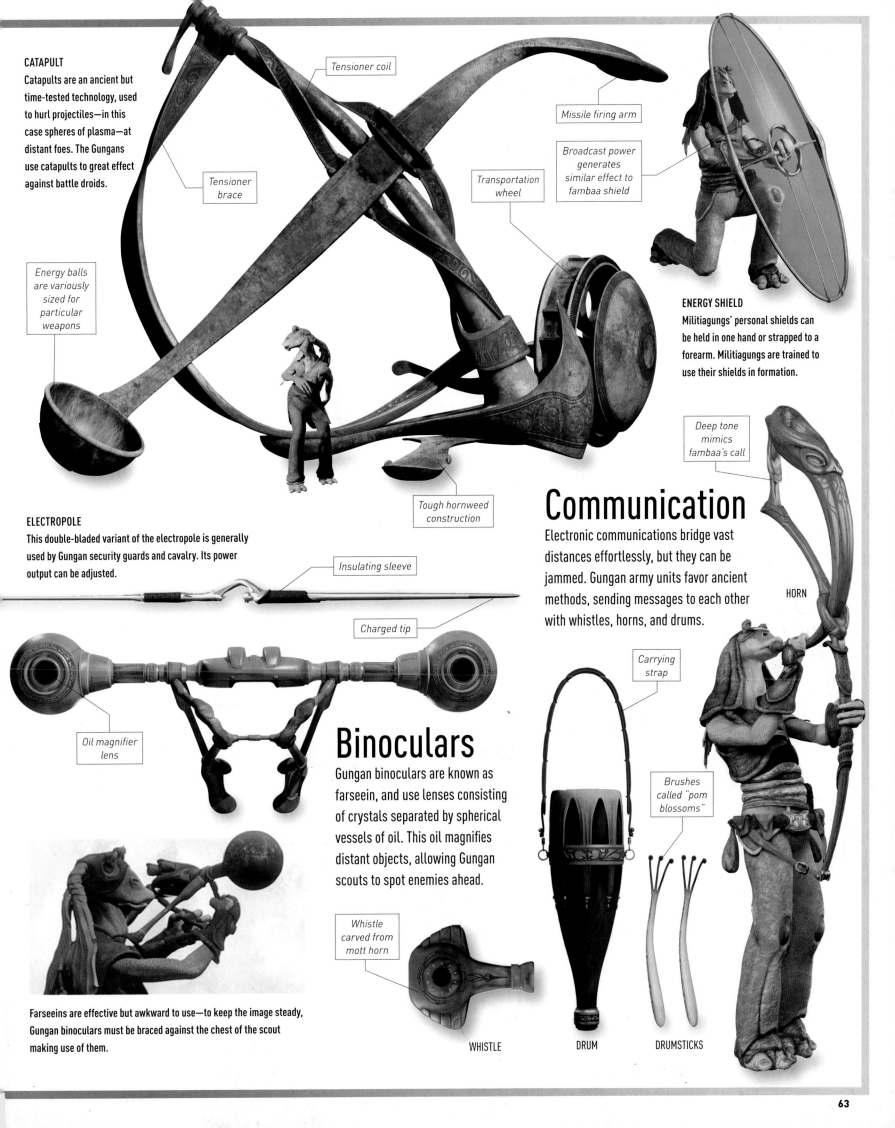

CATAPULT

Catapults are an ancient but time-tested technology, used to hurl projectiles—in this case spheres of plasma—at distant foes. The Gungans use catapults to great effect against battle droids.

Tensioner coil

Tensioner brace

Missile firing arm

Broadcast power generates similar effect to fambaa shield

Transportation wheel

Energy balls are variously sized for particular weapons

Tough hornweed construction

ENERGY SHIELD

Militiagungs' personal shields can be held in one hand or strapped to a forearm. Militiagungs are trained to use their shields in formation.

Deep tone mimics fambaa's call

ELECTROPOLE

This double-bladed variant of the electropole is generally used by Gungan security guards and cavalry. Its power output can be adjusted.

Insulating sleeve

Charged tip

Communication

Electronic communications bridge vast distances effortlessly, but they can be jammed. Gungan army units favor ancient methods, sending messages to each other with whistles, horns, and drums.

HORN

Oil magnifier lens

Carrying strap

Binoculars

Gungan binoculars are known as farseein, and use lenses consisting of crystals separated by spherical vessels of oil. This oil magnifies distant objects, allowing Gungan scouts to spot enemies ahead.

Brushes called "pom blossoms"

Whistle carved from mott horn

Farseeins are effective but awkward to use—to keep the image steady, Gungan binoculars must be braced against the chest of the scout making use of them.

WHISTLE

DRUM

DRUMSTICKS

Kaadu

Kaadu were domesticated long ago by Gungans who then lived on the surface of Naboo. They are primarily adapted for land-dwelling but can also breathe underwater for long periods. Kaadu decorated with giant feathers serve as agile mounts for Gungan soldiers and scouts.

Giant goff bird feathers

Saddlehorn

Fambaa trainers are among the most revered members of the Gungan armies. They must train these great beasts to stay in proper formation and remain steady amid the noise and terror of battle.

Energy distributor

Drum assembly receives beam from energy emitter and generates shield

Overload discharge spine

Saddle mount distributes weight of drum assembly

Fambaa Shield

Pairs of giant fambaa swamp lizards carry the Gungans' shield apparatus. A shield energy emitter mounted on the forward fambaa fires into the projector carried on the fambaa behind, producing a spherical shield-effect impervious to almost any bombardment. The Grand Army is protected inside this shield.

Drum assembly is mostly hollow

Drum fambaa aligns with beam fambaa in front

DRUM FAMBAA FRONT VIEW

DATA FILE

▶▶ **Fambaa shield generators** heat up when under fire and can be used only for a limited time under heavy attack.

▶▶ **Falumpasets are useful** for pulling battle wagons in war, and as ceremonial mounts during peacetime parades.

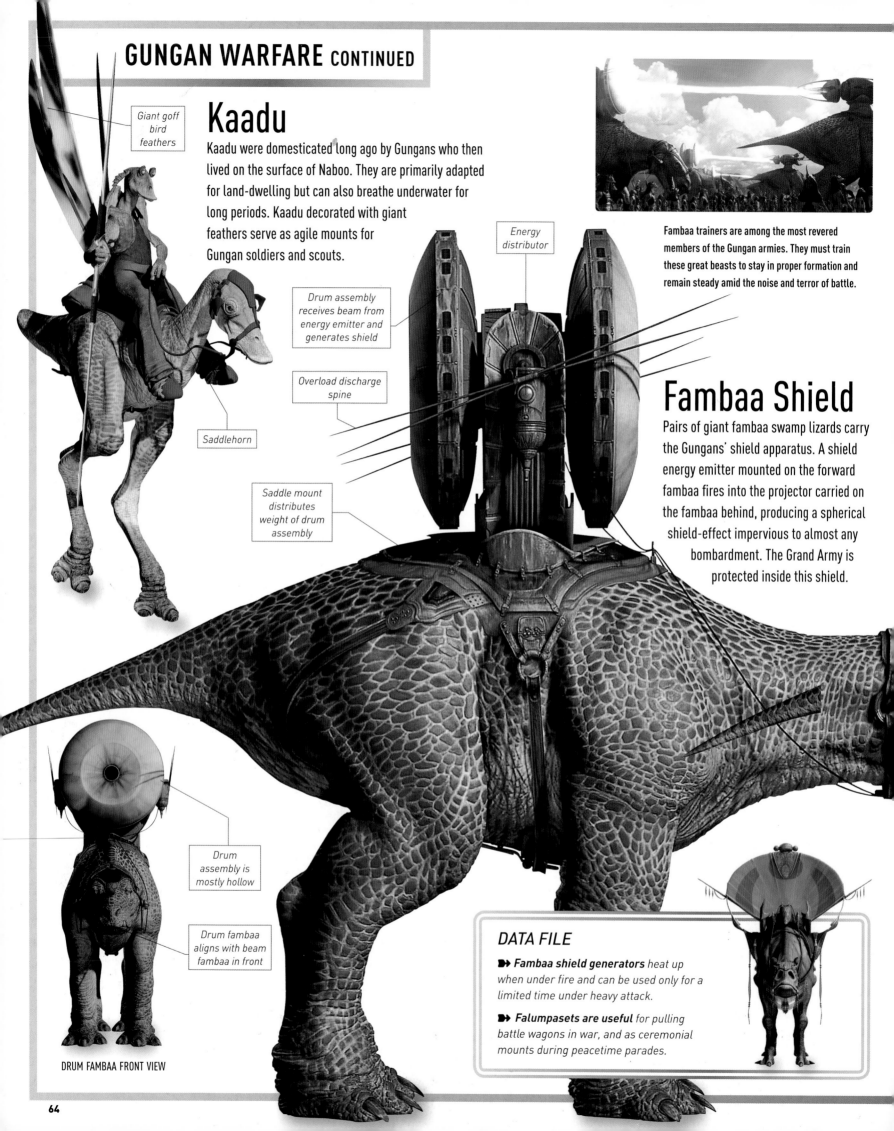

Battle Wagon

Using large wheels to minimize jolts, Gungan battle wagons carry supplies or racks of energy-ball ammunition to the combat line.

Battle wagon pulled by a hardy falumpaset

Long legs for crossing grasslands

Jar Jar discovers a unique defensive strategy at the Great Grassy Plains Battle: Racing to catch up with a battle wagon, he accidentally opens the rear gate, releasing energy balls that immobilize pursuing battle droids.

Electrically isolated operator cockpit

Overload discharge prongs

Shield energy emitter

Ion feed sostor

Static energy accumulation vanes

CONTROLLING THE SHIELD
An insulated cockpit at the front of the shield generator assembly protects operators from dangerous electrical energy. From here they direct the generator beam toward the projector drum.

Operator sits facing the drum

Heavy musculature

Reins

Bridle harness reinforces obedience

Saddle mount strap

Pillar-like legs keep high-energy shield projector well above army height

Waterproof skin

Multiple Gungan fambaa shields unite to form an enormous defensive bubble. However, the shield is not impervious to slow-moving enemy troops and the Trade Federation battle droids soon break through.

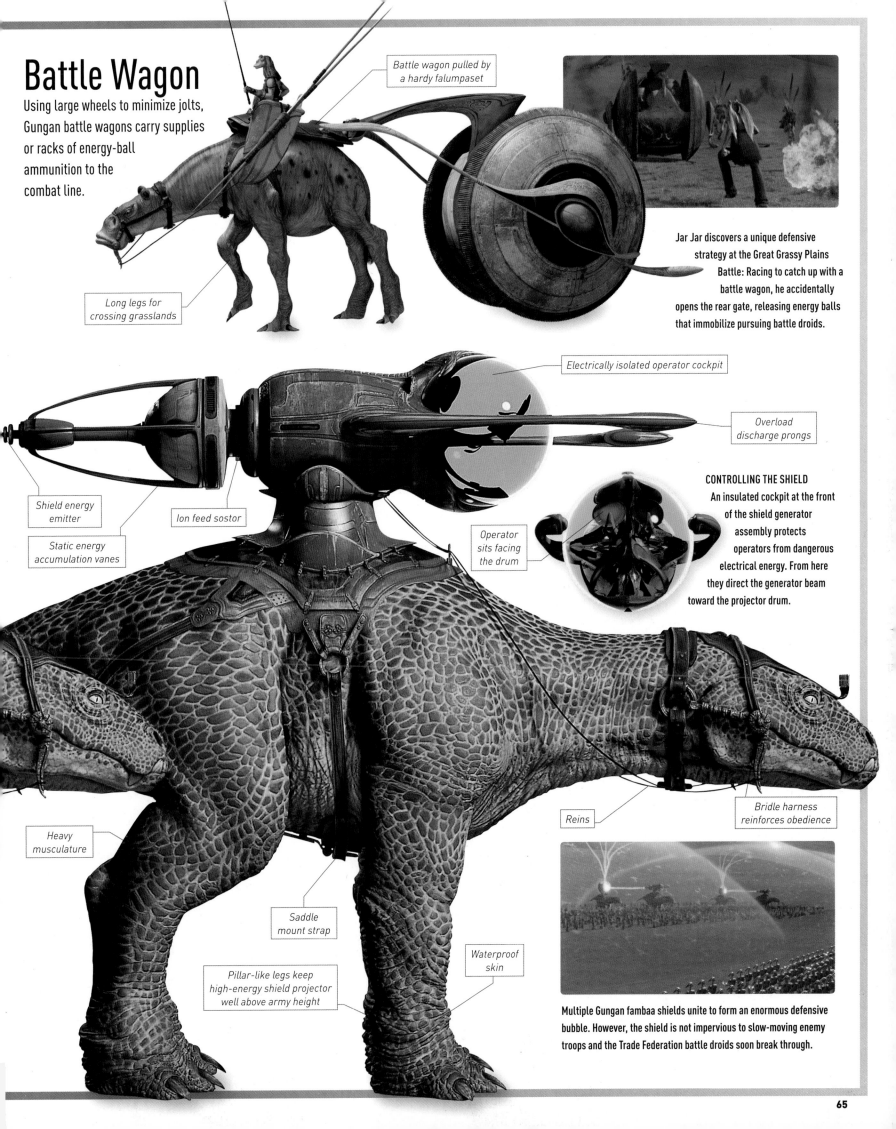

SEA MONSTERS OF NABOO

Otoh Gunga's inhabitants use Gungan subs to carry cargo and passengers through the Abyss: the labyrinthine undersea passages through Naboo's core. Boss Nass lends Qui-Gon and Obi-Wan a sub for their journey—but he also gives them Jar Jar as a "navigator."

THE WATERS OF NABOO ARE RICH WITH LIFE, THE BALANCE of sunlight and nutrients being ideal for many life forms. Microscopic plankton flourish in prodigious numbers, supporting a food chain that reaches its peak in giant predators. The sea monsters of Naboo are primarily lurkers of the deep, but some are known to drift to the surface at night or during storms—making ship travel a proverbially bad idea on the planet. Some of these monstrous creatures have been known to prey upon Gungan cities in oddly coordinated attacks, which is partly why the Gungan army stands in continued readiness. Repellent fields keep the leviathans away from the cities most of the time, but for still unexplained reasons one occasionally swims through.

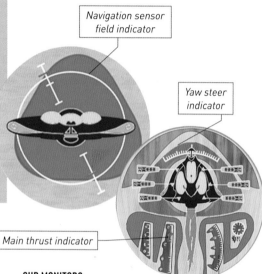

Navigation sensor field indicator

Yaw steer indicator

Main thrust indicator

Yaw thrust indicator

SUB MONITORS
Even a novice pilot can handle a Gungan sub, using its monitors as eyes and ears and taking hold of the craft's simple, highly responsive controls.

Colo Claw Fish

This serpentine predator is adapted to swallow prey larger than its own head. Its jaws can distend and its skin can stretch to engulf astonishingly large creatures. The colo seizes prey with the huge pectoral claws for which it is named, having initially disoriented it by uttering a weird hydrosonic shriek using special structures in its throat and head. The colo digests its food slowly using weak stomach acids and must be certain to stun its prey with its venomous fangs before swallowing to avoid the creature eating its way out of the colo to safety.

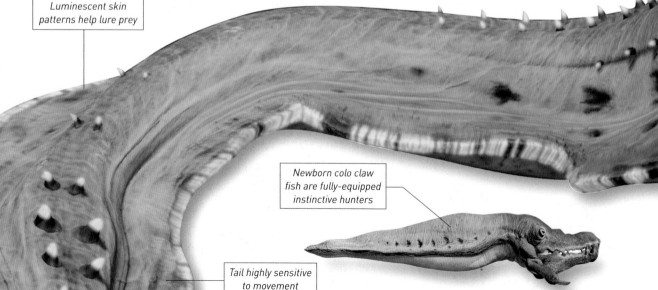

Luminescent skin patterns help lure prey

Newborn colo claw fish are fully-equipped instinctive hunters

Tail highly sensitive to movement

BABY COLO CLAW FISH
Female colo claw fish chase off males after mating to prevent them from eating the eggs and hatchlings. Young colos face other predators: Gungans and the Naboo both consider their tender flesh a delicacy.

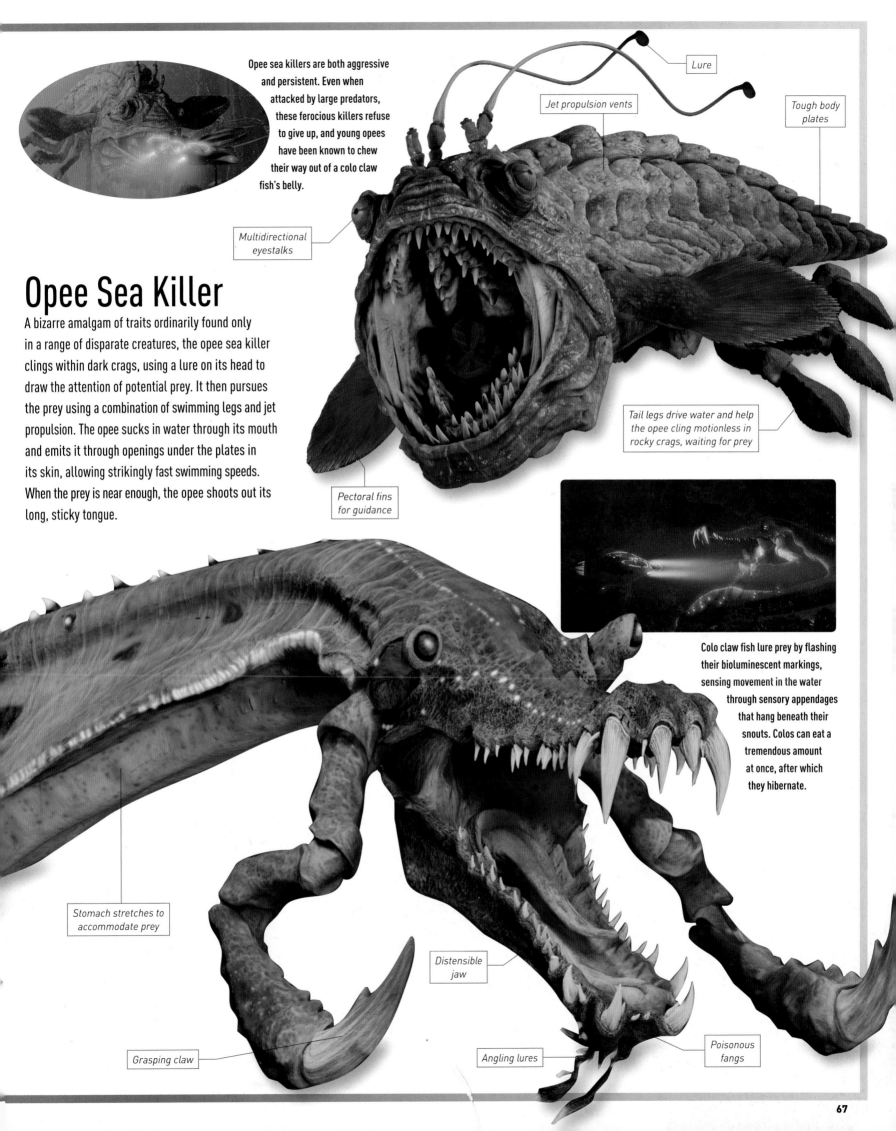

Opee sea killers are both aggressive and persistent. Even when attacked by large predators, these ferocious killers refuse to give up, and young opees have been known to chew their way out of a colo claw fish's belly.

Lure

Jet propulsion vents

Tough body plates

Multidirectional eyestalks

Opee Sea Killer

A bizarre amalgam of traits ordinarily found only in a range of disparate creatures, the opee sea killer clings within dark crags, using a lure on its head to draw the attention of potential prey. It then pursues the prey using a combination of swimming legs and jet propulsion. The opee sucks in water through its mouth and emits it through openings under the plates in its skin, allowing strikingly fast swimming speeds. When the prey is near enough, the opee shoots out its long, sticky tongue.

Tail legs drive water and help the opee cling motionless in rocky crags, waiting for prey

Pectoral fins for guidance

Colo claw fish lure prey by flashing their bioluminescent markings, sensing movement in the water through sensory appendages that hang beneath their snouts. Colos can eat a tremendous amount at once, after which they hibernate.

Stomach stretches to accommodate prey

Distensible jaw

Grasping claw

Angling lures

Poisonous fangs

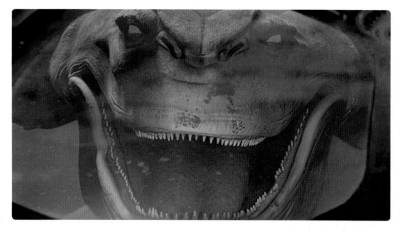

Investigating the habits of the sando aqua monster would be a highly dangerous undertaking, even using the most advanced defensive equipment. The sando appears without warning and can swallow most other sea dwellers in a single gulp. Sensible ecologists prefer to study the predators from the safety of a lab, using droid explorer craft in the water.

DATA FILE

➤ **The Abyss's ecosystem** depends on abundant plankton and smaller fish. Larger predators are quite rare—though that is little comfort to Obi-Wan, Qui-Gon, and Jar Jar on their eventful trip to Theed.

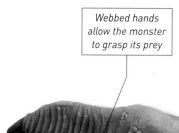

Webbed hands allow the monster to grasp its prey

The opee sea killer's armored body protects it against most underwater predators, but it is defenseless against the powerful jaws of giant leviathans such as the sando aqua monster. Sandos have been known to emerge from Naboo's swampy shallows to gobble up herds of fambaas and falumpasets on land.

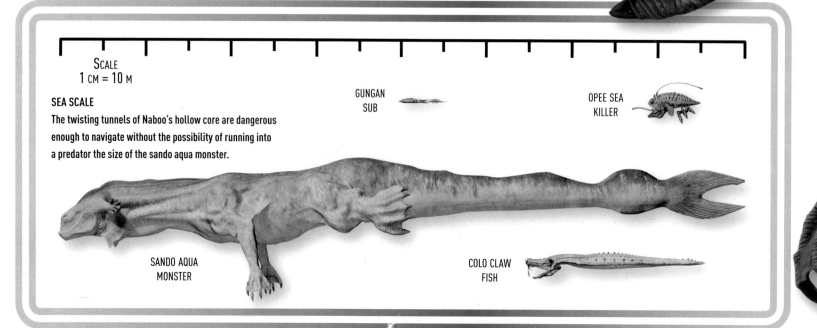

SCALE
1 CM = 10 M

SEA SCALE
The twisting tunnels of Naboo's hollow core are dangerous enough to navigate without the possibility of running into a predator the size of the sando aqua monster.

GUNGAN
SUB

OPEE SEA
KILLER

SANDO AQUA
MONSTER

COLO CLAW
FISH

Long tail provides propulsion

Sando kits nurse from teats on belly

Organs of unknown purpose at end of tail

Rayed tail flukes

Delicate dorsal fins detect movement in water

Gills

Muscular body not smoothed by fat or blubber, and not fully adapted to swimming

Non-streamlined head evidence of land-based ancestor

Strong jaws for powerful bite

Razor sharp teeth line the jaw

Claws for digging up giant crustaceans of the Abyss

Sando Aqua Monster

The most fabled of Naboo's sea nightmares, the sando aqua monster is rarely seen. In spite of its awesome size, it is somehow capable of hiding in deep environments. The sando aqua monster's arms and legs are only partly adapted into flippers, which suggests that its recent ancestors must have been land creatures. How this gargantuan beast eats enough to support its body functions remains to be explained—as does much of Naboo's ecology.

DARTH MAUL

THE TATTOOED WARRIOR DARTH MAUL KNOWS HIS HISTORY.
A thousand years ago the Jedi Order ended the Sith's glorious dominion, forcing the followers of the dark side into hiding. But now, things are changing... Maul has absorbed his Master Darth Sidious's lessons and has learned to command the power of the dark side so that he may carry out the Sith Lord's orders. Sidious's endgame has begun, and Maul is at last free to confront the Jedi and destroy them. The Sith believe that they will soon reign supreme once more, with Sidious as unquestioned ruler of the galaxy. And eventually, when Sidious has nothing more to teach, Maul may plot against his Master to take his place.

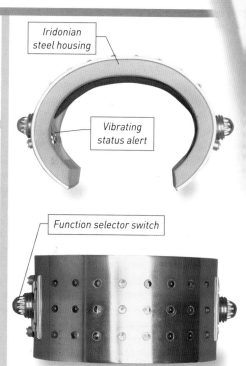

Iridonian steel housing

Vibrating status alert

Function selector switch

Maul has performed many missions for Sidious, from tracking down Trade Federation turncoats to helping bring the galaxy's crimelords under the Sith Lord's control. He obeys his Master's commands without question, content (for now) to serve as an instrument of his will.

Maul prides himself on his abilities as a tracker, and relishes the challenge of difficult assignments given to him by his Sith Master.

Wrist Link

Maul's programmable wrist link allows him to remotely direct probe droids, arm traps, detonate bombs, and conduct other treacherous activities. It also receives signals from surveillance devices.

Electrobinoculars

On Tatooine, Maul uses electrobinoculars to search for the Jedi. These electrobinoculars are equipped with radiation sensors for night vision and powerful light-gathering components for long-distance scanning.

Power cells

Light-gathering lens

Multi-scan controls

Function controls

Transmission and reception antenna

ELECTROBINOCULAR VIEWSCREEN

Tied to global mapping scanners in his starship, Maul's electrobinocular viewscreen displays the precise location of targets and indicates life signals or power frequencies. Specific shapes, colors, or energy types can be set as targets, and even invisible defensive fields can be detected.

Memory stores 360° horizon view

Filters screen out atmospheric interference

Nav-grid can be projected onto landscape

Alarm signals energy sources or visual targets

Mode indicator

Range to target

Magnification

DATA FILE

▶▶ **Maul is a master** of physical combat, pairing Orsis Academy elite combat training with the fighting style of Teräs Käsi and lightsaber disciplines Niman, Jar'Kai, and Dun Möch.

▶▶ **Sith tracker beacons** allow Darth Sidious's agents to monitor communications by the Sith Lord's enemies.

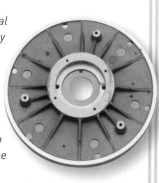

Sith Apprentice

Darth Maul is one of the most highly trained Sith in the history of the order. Focusing on physical and tactical abilities, Maul serves his Master obediently, believing that his own time for strategic wisdom and eventual domination will come. His face is tattooed with symbols giving evidence of his complete dedication to discipline in the dark side.

Vestigial horns

Hairless skull

Nightbrother tattoos

Gleaming yellow eyes

Dark robe

Double-bladed lightsaber

Beam emitter

Field cloak cut to allow fighting movement

Lightsaber blade is red due to nature of internal crystals

Heavy-action boots

Transmission antenna

External weapons mount

Magnetic imaging device

Scan-absorbing stealth shell

Primary photoreceptor

Gauntlets

Levitator

Thermal imager

Probe Droid

Darth Maul uses a lot of elaborate technology in his work as the Sith apprentice of Darth Sidious, but one of his most useful tools is the "Dark Eye" (DRK-1) probe droid—a hovering reconnaissance device that can be programmed to seek out individuals or information.

Ball detonator

Scanning lens attachment

"DARK EYE" DEVICES
Probe droids locate their quarry using multispectral imaging and many kinds of scanning. The probes silently monitor conversations and eavesdrop on electronic transmissions, and can be fitted with a number of small, deadly weapons.

INTERNAL VIEW

Arakyd Industries builds DRK-1 probes according to plans that are more than a millennium old, derived from one of Darth Sidious's many Sith holocrons.

Repulsorlift actuator

Thermal-imager data feed

DARTH MAUL CONTINUED

The *Scimitar*

Darth Maul's Sith Infiltrator is a heavily customized Star Courier produced by the brilliant engineer Raith Sienar. It incorporates an experimental ion engine system and a rare cloaking device which renders Maul's ship invisible to organic eyes as well as mechanical sensors when activated. The design—provided by Darth Sidious—echoes craft from the ancient Sith Empire.

SIDE VIEW

Aft landing skid

Laser cannons

Sublight engines

Crew cabin seats seven

Bat wings fold inwards

Blade arc tip

Cloaking-field generator

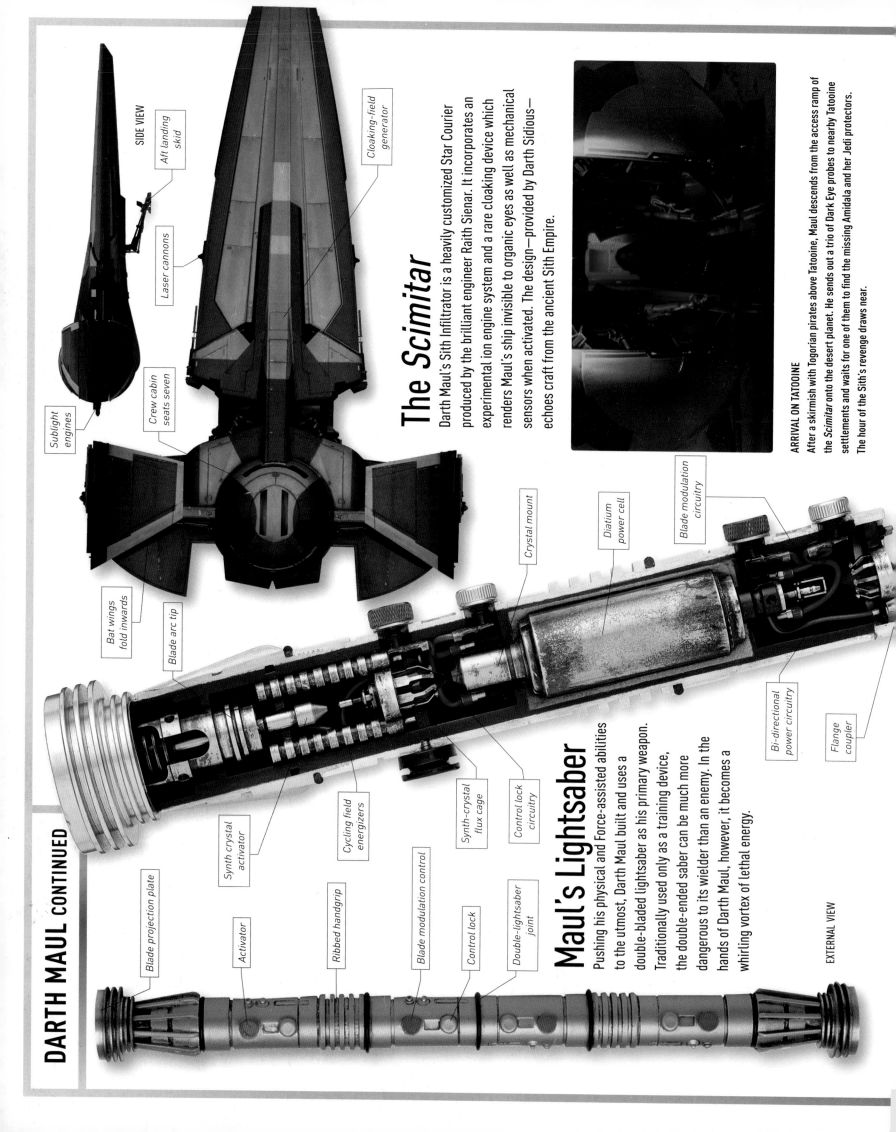

ARRIVAL ON TATOOINE
After a skirmish with Togorian pirates above Tatooine, Maul descends from the access ramp of the *Scimitar* onto the desert planet. He sends out a trio of Dark Eye probes to nearby Tatooine settlements and waits for one of them to find the missing Amidala and her Jedi protectors. The hour of the Sith's revenge draws near.

Maul's Lightsaber

Pushing his physical and Force-assisted abilities to the utmost, Darth Maul built and uses a double-bladed lightsaber as his primary weapon. Traditionally used only as a training device, the double-ended saber can be much more dangerous to its wielder than an enemy. In the hands of Darth Maul, however, it becomes a whirling vortex of lethal energy.

Crystal mount

Diatium power cell

Blade modulation circuitry

Bi-directional power circuitry

Flange coupler

Synth crystal activator

Cycling field energizers

Synth-crystal flux cage

Control lock circuitry

Blade projection plate

Activator

Ribbed handgrip

Blade modulation control

Control lock

Double-lightsaber joint

EXTERNAL VIEW

With his double-bladed lightsaber, Maul is equal to two Jedi who are unprepared for his powers. Since the Sith disappeared almost 1,000 years ago, Jedi are not used to facing opponents with lightsabers.

SABERSTAFF

Double-bladed sabers are rare, but both Jedi and Sith have used them as weapons over the millennia. Maul's effectively conjoins two sabers within one housing, with each blade containing two crystals: a central synth-crystal and a secondary synth-crystal for additional power. His saberstaff's design was influenced by an ancient Zabrak weapon known as a zhaboka.

Secondary synth-crystal

Accelerator

Primary synth crystal

Thin layer of power insulation

Repulsorlift

FRONT VIEW

Control linkages

Open cockpit design offers optimum visibility

Acceleration handgrips

Steering bar

Braking pedal

Darth Maul's speeder is powered by a strong repulsorlift engine for rapid acceleration and sharp cornering. The *Bloodfin* has no weapons: Maul considers blasters uncivilized, preferring to assault his enemies face-to-face with a Sith blade or to eliminate them through treachery. The open-cockpit design allows Maul to leap directly from the speeder into battle.

The *Bloodfin*

The Sith draw their power from the Force, but utilize technological tools where the Jedi prefer to shun them. Maul's custom Razalon FC-20 speeder bike allows him to race off in pursuit of his enemies and confront them saber to saber. It has a very low center of gravity, which helps give it superb cornering ability.

SHMI SKYWALKER

WHEN PIRATES CAPTURED HER PARENTS DURING A SPACE voyage in the Outer Rim, young Shmi Skywalker was sold into slavery and separated from her family. During a difficult childhood, Shmi was taken from one system to another by several masters of various species while serving as a house servant. When no longer a girl, Shmi was dropped from house servant status and was forced into cleaning work. Although slavery is illegal in the Republic, laws do not reach all parts of the galaxy—and while inexpensive droids can perform menial tasks as well as humans, living slaves give great status and prestige to their owners.

Rough-spun tunic withstands harsh Tatooine weather

Simple hairstyle typical of servants

Decorative belt

Mladong bracelet

SHMI'S KITCHEN
In spite of their poverty, Shmi works hard to make a good home for herself and her son, Anakin. Her kitchen includes some labor-saving devices, but lacks the more costly moisture-conserving domes and fields, which help save precious—and expensive—water.

Spicy ahrisa

Lamta

Tezirett seed

Sidi gourd

MOS ESPA PRODUCE

Haroun bread

Driss pod

WORKSTATION
When Shmi is not working at Watto's home, she is permitted to clean computer memory devices to bring in a modest income. A small area in their home where Shmi keeps her tools and equipment is devoted to this activity.

Repulsor hood

Magnifier

Illuminator rings

AEROMAGNIFIER
Some of the tools at Shmi's workstation were given to Shmi in recognition of her service as a dependable servant. When Watto obtained an aeromagnifier in a large lot of used goods, he gave it to Shmi even though he could have sold it. The magnifier hovers in the right position to help her see what she is working on.

Slave and Mother
Tantalized several times by the false possibility of freedom, Shmi now accepts her life and finds joy in her son Anakin, whom she loves dearly. Shmi and Anakin live together in the Slave Quarter of Mos Espa, a collection of adobe hovels piled together at the edge of town.

When the Jedi Master Qui-Gon Jinn recognizes Anakin's special qualities and offers to take him away to a greater destiny, only Shmi's selfless care for her son gives her the strength to let him go.

DATA FILE
➤ **Shmi learned her** technical skills under a former master, Pi-Lippa, who planned to grant Shmi her freedom. However, when Pi-Lippa died Shmi was sold to a relative.

➤ **Shmi can always** sense when Anakin is nearby, even when she cannot see or hear him.

ANAKIN SKYWALKER

ALTHOUGH HE LOOKS LIKE ANY OTHER NINE-YEAR-OLD BOY living on the Outer Rim planet of Tatooine, Anakin Skywalker is far from ordinary. A slave to the junk dealer Watto, Anakin lives with his mother, in the spaceport city of Mos Espa. He has a natural ability with mechanical devices, quickly understanding how they work. In his spare time, Anakin repairs and builds machines, including Podracer engines and a working droid. Qui-Gon Jinn notices his keen perception and unnaturally fast reflexes, and recognizes that the Force is extraordinarily strong in Anakin.

Slave's simple haircut

Necklace given to Anakin by his mother

Arm wraps

Rough work clothing

Leg wraps keep out sand

Slave and Dreamer

Anakin has been raised by his mother to believe in himself. She has given him faith in his dreams in spite of their humble situation as slaves. Anakin looks forward to the day when he will be free to pilot starships of the mainline through the spacelanes of the galaxy. He soon finds that belief in one's dreams can have powerful results.

ANAKIN'S BEDROOM
Anakin has his own room in the Skywalker home. Electronic and mechanical components are piled around his bed since Anakin is constantly tinkering and trying to figure things out. Working for Watto gives Anakin the chance to pick up scrap equipment here and there.

Among Anakin's friends is Wald, a young Rodian who speaks Huttese. Wald doubts Anakin's extraordinary abilities.

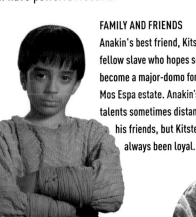

KITSTER

FAMILY AND FRIENDS
Anakin's best friend, Kitster, is a fellow slave who hopes someday to become a major-domo for a wealthy Mos Espa estate. Anakin's unusual talents sometimes distance him from his friends, but Kitster has always been loyal.

MELEÉ

Owned by Gardulla the Hutt, Meleé is a capable mechanic, though not as skilled as Anakin Skywalker.

DATA FILE

➡ **Anakin once belonged** to Gardulla the Hutt, but she lost him in a bet to Watto when Anakin was about three years old.

Tool pouch

Survival flares for use in sandstorms

TRAVEL PACK
Leaving for Coruscant, Anakin takes clothes, tools, and a few keepsakes from Tatooine.

Cheap, durable jumba leather

FROM PILOT TO JEDI

PODRACING DEMANDS LIGHTNING-FAST REFLEXES AND A
superb feel for machines, which makes the sport a perfect fit for young Anakin
Skywalker. Human Podracers are all but unknown: They lack fast reflexes, multiple limbs,
durable bodies, and other necessities for competition. But young Anakin is exceptional in a
number of ways: His reaction time is far better than that of a normal human, and he has a
genius for rethinking and re-engineering mechanical systems. Watto has noticed the boy's
skills, and dreams that his slave will one day bring him a rich payday and elevate him in the
gambling-mad society of Mos Espa slaveowners. Anakin loves Podracing for different
reasons: While hurtling across Tatooine at 800 kph, he has no time to brood about life as a
slave on a desert world. Behind the controls of a Podracer, he feels free.

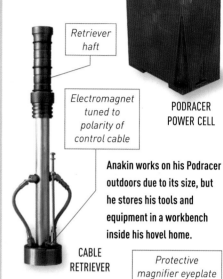

Connection plate

PODRACER POWER CELL

Retriever haft

Electromagnet tuned to polarity of control cable

Anakin works on his Podracer outdoors due to its size, but he stores his tools and equipment in a workbench inside his hovel home.

CABLE RETRIEVER

Protective magnifier eyeplate

WELDING GOGGLES

Podracer Engineer

Anakin understands the workings of Podracers from
helping mechanics and pit droids repair them for
Watto. When Anakin took a repaired Podracer for a
test spin, Watto was furious, but he was also
amazed at the boy's reflexes. Soon, the test drives
turned into qualifying laps, and Anakin became a
Podracer pilot despite his age.

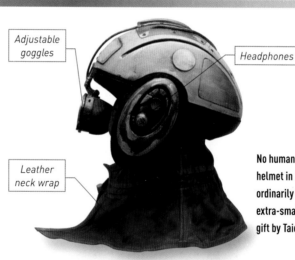

Adjustable goggles

Headphones

Leather neck wrap

No human has ever needed a Podracing
helmet in Mos Espa, since humans
ordinarily cannot ride Podracers. Anakin's
extra-small helmet was made for him as a
gift by Taieb, a local craftsman.

Control cable

Control Pod

Thrust stabilizer cone

Anakin has secretly restored and rebuilt a junked Podracer
using parts Watto didn't think could be salvaged, and
others obtained from Jawa traders. Anakin and Qui-Gon
convince Watto that the Podracer is Qui-Gon's and enter
it in the notorious Boonta Eve Classic Podrace.

Repulsorlift

Air scoops act as
steering brakes

Radon-Ulzer
engines

DATA FILE

➡ **As a nine-year-old**
boy, Anakin would never
be allowed to compete in
civilized Podraces, but
the Outer Rim is known
for its exciting free-for-
all race policies.

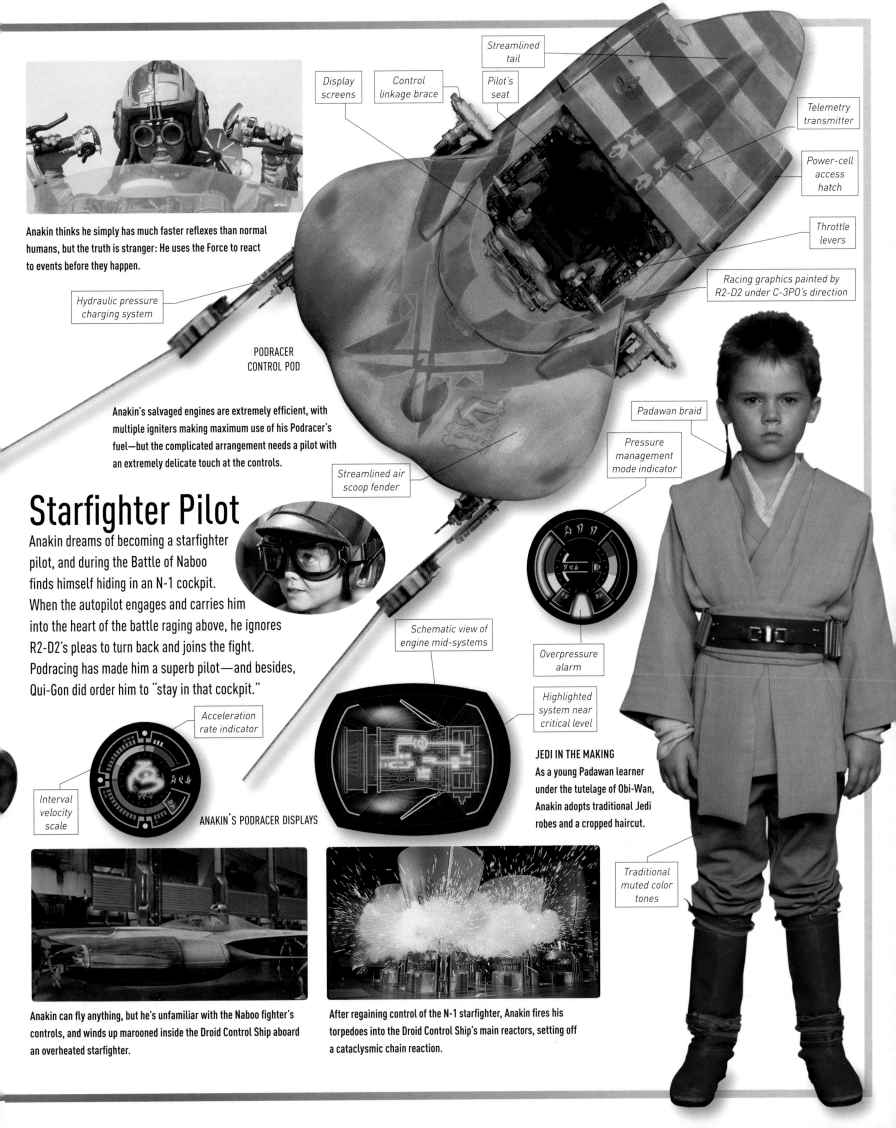

Anakin thinks he simply has much faster reflexes than normal humans, but the truth is stranger: He uses the Force to react to events before they happen.

Hydraulic pressure charging system

PODRACER CONTROL POD

Display screens

Control linkage brace

Pilot's seat

Streamlined tail

Telemetry transmitter

Power-cell access hatch

Throttle levers

Racing graphics painted by R2-D2 under C-3PO's direction

Anakin's salvaged engines are extremely efficient, with multiple igniters making maximum use of his Podracer's fuel—but the complicated arrangement needs a pilot with an extremely delicate touch at the controls.

Streamlined air scoop fender

Padawan braid

Pressure management mode indicator

Starfighter Pilot

Anakin dreams of becoming a starfighter pilot, and during the Battle of Naboo finds himself hiding in an N-1 cockpit. When the autopilot engages and carries him into the heart of the battle raging above, he ignores R2-D2's pleas to turn back and joins the fight. Podracing has made him a superb pilot—and besides, Qui-Gon did order him to "stay in that cockpit."

Overpressure alarm

Schematic view of engine mid-systems

Highlighted system near critical level

Acceleration rate indicator

Interval velocity scale

ANAKIN'S PODRACER DISPLAYS

JEDI IN THE MAKING
As a young Padawan learner under the tutelage of Obi-Wan, Anakin adopts traditional Jedi robes and a cropped haircut.

Traditional muted color tones

Anakin can fly anything, but he's unfamiliar with the Naboo fighter's controls, and winds up marooned inside the Droid Control Ship aboard an overheated starfighter.

After regaining control of the N-1 starfighter, Anakin fires his torpedoes into the Droid Control Ship's main reactors, setting off a cataclysmic chain reaction.

C-3PO

STANDARD CYBOT GALACTICA

Protocol droids have been in use for generations. When Anakin found the structural elements of a droid that had been stripped of parts, he restored it as a helper for his mother. Over time, Anakin scrounged the parts to complete his droid, fabricating many components himself. Anakin's droid lacks a "skin" since droid plating is valuable and the boy cannot afford it. The droid, whose designation is C-3PO, has yet to realize that his parts are showing.

Antique Droid

Identification glyphs on C-3PO's parts indicate he was built in Cybot Galactica's great foundries on the famed factory world of Affa. In that era Cybot Galactica built droids to last—Anakin needed to replace or repair a number of things, but knew C-3PO could be made functional again.

A protocol droid offers no obvious benefit to a household of Mos Espa slaves, but Anakin figures C-3PO can help Shmi and run errands. Doesn't even a wrecked droid deserve a chance?

Photoreceptors

Droid photoreceptors can be extremely sophisticated, allowing mechanicals to see across the entire spectrum or use their eyes as microscopes or telescopes. Protocol droids, however, possess only baseline visual acuity and when Anakin finds C-3PO, his photoreceptors are burned-out.

Anakin switched C-3PO's dead photoreceptors for those of a used droid bought by Watto, which can now barely see. When Watto wonders how the half-blind droid managed to walk into his shop in the first place, Anakin shrugs. It's a mysterious galaxy.

Photoreceptor modulation impulse carrier

Image component lines

Signal component collector pins

Photoreceptor mount frame

Image signal transmitter

Composite image integrator

Active sensing elements

PHOTORECEPTOR FRONT VIEW

Photoreceptor elements

Balance gyro

Borrowed photoreceptors

Vocoder plate

Movement sensor wiring

Flexible mid-body section

Main power recharge socket

Pelvic joint

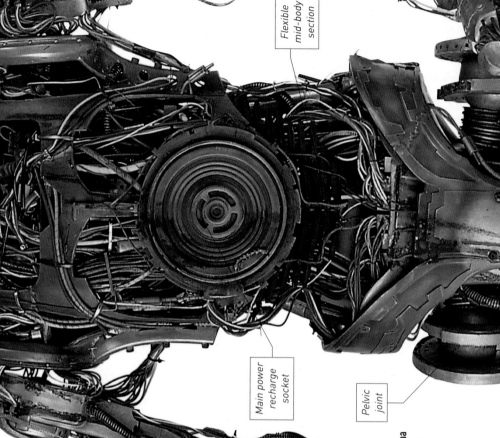

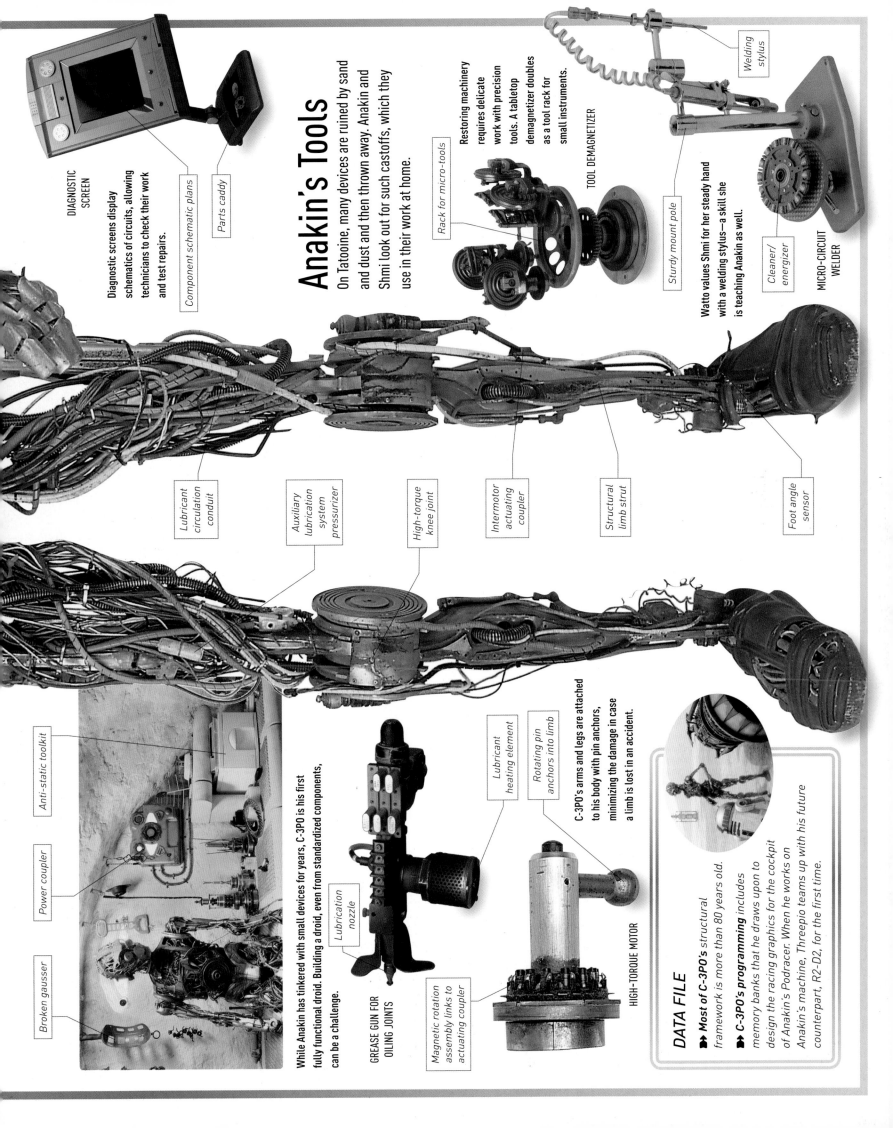

Anakin's Tools

On Tatooine, many devices are ruined by sand and dust and then thrown away. Anakin and Shmi look out for such castoffs, which they use in their work at home.

DIAGNOSTIC SCREEN

Diagnostic screens display schematics of circuits, allowing technicians to check their work and test repairs.

Component schematic plans

Parts caddy

Rack for micro-tools

Restoring machinery requires delicate work with precision tools. A tabletop demagnetizer doubles as a tool rack for small instruments.

TOOL DEMAGNETIZER

Welding stylus

Sturdy mount pole

Cleaner/ energizer

Watto values Shmi for her steady hand with a welding stylus—a skill she is teaching Anakin as well.

MICRO-CIRCUIT WELDER

Lubricant circulation conduit

Auxiliary lubrication system pressurizer

High-torque knee joint

Intermotor actuating coupler

Structural limb strut

Foot angle sensor

Anti-static toolkit

Power coupler

Broken gausser

While Anakin has tinkered with small devices for years, C-3PO is his first fully functional droid. Building a droid, even from standardized components, can be a challenge.

Lubrication nozzle

GREASE GUN FOR OILING JOINTS

Magnetic rotation assembly links to actuating coupler

Lubricant heating element

Rotating pin anchors into limb

C-3PO's arms and legs are attached to his body with pin anchors, minimizing the damage in case a limb is lost in an accident.

HIGH-TORQUE MOTOR

DATA FILE

▶▶ **Most of C-3PO's** structural framework is more than 80 years old.

▶▶ **C-3PO's programming** includes memory banks that he draws upon to design the racing graphics for the cockpit of Anakin's Podracer. When he works on Anakin's machine, Threepio teams up with his future counterpart, R2-D2, for the first time.

WATTO

SHREWD AND POSSESSIVE, WATTO IS THE OWNER OF A
parts shop in the Tatooine frontier town of Mos Espa. A flying Toydarian with
rapidly-beating wings, Watto's pudgy body is not as heavy as it looks due to his
spongy, gas-filled tissues. The junk dealer has a sharp eye for a bargain, and knows
equipment merchandise inside and out. Success has allowed Watto to indulge his
passion for gambling. He regularly places large bets on Mos Espa's famous Podrace
competitions, matching his wits and money against the Hutts, who control the
gambling world. In the past, such bets have won Watto many slaves—prized
possessions and trophies of his acumen.

In the rugged frontier society of the Outer Rim, only hard currency
counts. When Qui-Gon shows up hoping to pay with Republic credits,
Watto only laughs.

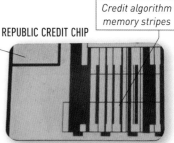

Security codeout

REPUBLIC CREDIT CHIP

Credit algorithm
memory stripes

WUPIUPI (TATOOINE COINS)

Watto's Junkshop

Although Watto insists that his establishment is
a parts dealership, everyone else calls it a junk
shop. It cannot be denied that the range of
merchandise runs from desirable rare parts and
working droids to unusable scrap that he would
have a hard time unloading even on desperate
Jawas. Watto's droids, slaves, and staff
perform repairs, obtain parts needed by
clients, and do custom work with a wide
range of mechanical devices.

Old-style sales
register device

Protocol droid
(missing some parts)

Miscellaneous scrap stuck to
short-range re-grav plate in ceiling

Pit droid

Power droids
handy for
powering
up depleted
cells in
merchandise

Rough adobe
walls hide
coolant
circulating
layers

Hard memory
cycler (cleaned
by Shmi
Skywalker)

Illuminated
counter
surface

Electrostatic
damping
floor mats
keep sand
and dust
down

Monocular
photoreceptor

Equipment
interface panel

**Bizarre improvised
equipment can be found in
Watto's shop, such as the
Jawa R1-type drone that
assists with shopkeeping.**

Serving arms

Diagnostic hookup for testing
trade merchandise

Power Droid

Power droids of the GNK series are mobile generators that supply
power for machinery or other droids. They hover silently in the
background, so commonplace that they are hardly noticed.

Receptacle

Test
readouts

SERVING COUNTER
TEST PANELS

Control
switch

Monochromatic
photoreceptor

Polyfeed
power outlets

Ambulation
gear housing

Vocoder

TALKING MAGNETITE CLEANER

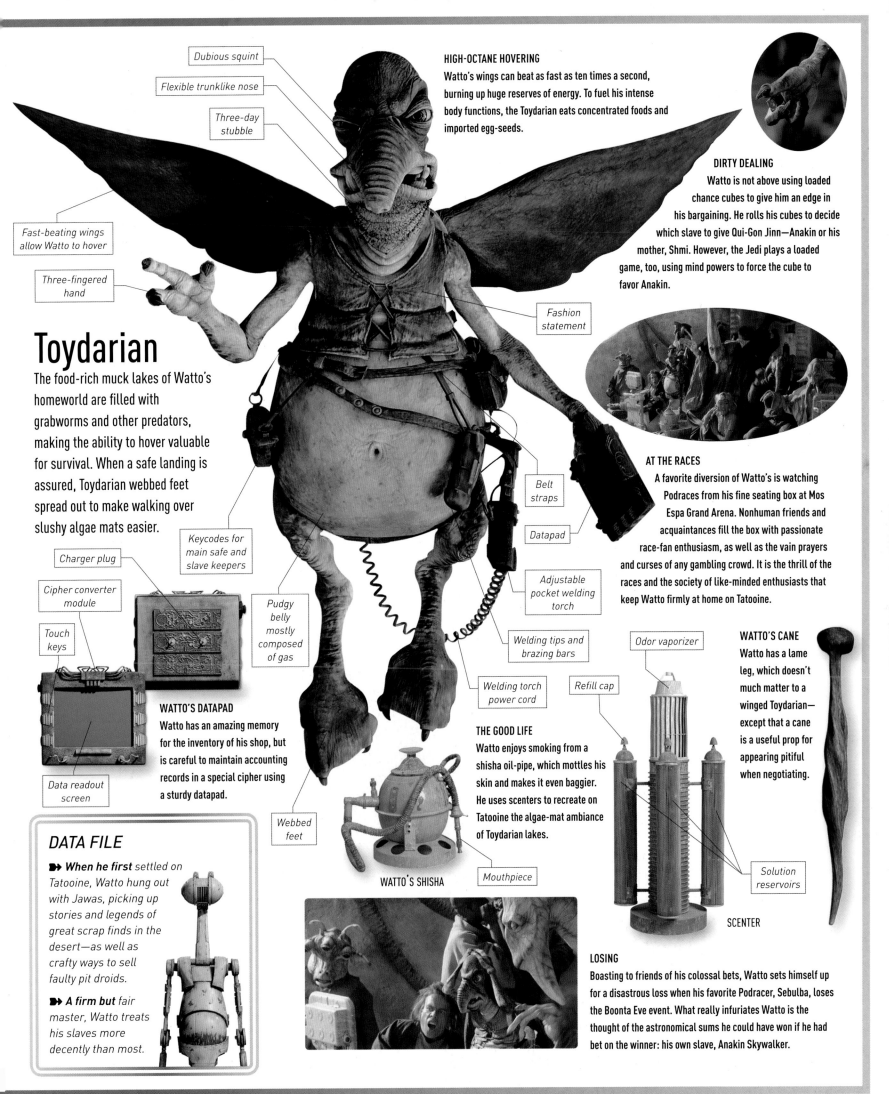

Dubious squint

Flexible trunklike nose

Three-day stubble

HIGH-OCTANE HOVERING
Watto's wings can beat as fast as ten times a second, burning up huge reserves of energy. To fuel his intense body functions, the Toydarian eats concentrated foods and imported egg-seeds.

Fast-beating wings allow Watto to hover

Three-fingered hand

DIRTY DEALING
Watto is not above using loaded chance cubes to give him an edge in his bargaining. He rolls his cubes to decide which slave to give Qui-Gon Jinn—Anakin or his mother, Shmi. However, the Jedi plays a loaded game, too, using mind powers to force the cube to favor Anakin.

Fashion statement

Toydarian
The food-rich muck lakes of Watto's homeworld are filled with grabworms and other predators, making the ability to hover valuable for survival. When a safe landing is assured, Toydarian webbed feet spread out to make walking over slushy algae mats easier.

Belt straps

Datapad

AT THE RACES
A favorite diversion of Watto's is watching Podraces from his fine seating box at Mos Espa Grand Arena. Nonhuman friends and acquaintances fill the box with passionate race-fan enthusiasm, as well as the vain prayers and curses of any gambling crowd. It is the thrill of the races and the society of like-minded enthusiasts that keep Watto firmly at home on Tatooine.

Keycodes for main safe and slave keepers

Charger plug

Cipher converter module

Touch keys

Pudgy belly mostly composed of gas

Adjustable pocket welding torch

Odor vaporizer

Refill cap

WATTO'S CANE
Watto has a lame leg, which doesn't much matter to a winged Toydarian—except that a cane is a useful prop for appearing pitiful when negotiating.

Welding tips and brazing bars

WATTO'S DATAPAD
Watto has an amazing memory for the inventory of his shop, but is careful to maintain accounting records in a special cipher using a sturdy datapad.

Data readout screen

Welding torch power cord

THE GOOD LIFE
Watto enjoys smoking from a shisha oil-pipe, which mottles his skin and makes it even baggier. He uses scenters to recreate on Tatooine the algae-mat ambiance of Toydarian lakes.

Webbed feet

Solution reservoirs

SCENTER

WATTO'S SHISHA

Mouthpiece

LOSING
Boasting to friends of his colossal bets, Watto sets himself up for a disastrous loss when his favorite Podracer, Sebulba, loses the Boonta Eve event. What really infuriates Watto is the thought of the astronomical sums he could have won if he had bet on the winner: his own slave, Anakin Skywalker.

SEBULBA

AMONG THE PODRACER PILOTS OF THE RUGGED OUTER
Rim circuit, Sebulba has accelerated his way to the top with an unbeatable combination of courage, skill, and outrageous cheating. His murderous tactics often bring his competitors down in flames, but he knows where the race cameras are placed and manages to avoid being seen. In spite of his crimes, Sebulba has found that in Mos Espa success makes its own rules. Now enjoying the power and prestige of being a top racer, the unscrupulous Dug has just one thorn in his side—the young Podracer named Anakin Skywalker.

Sebulba's anger towards Anakin stems chiefly from fear. If the young human were ever to win a race, even by accident, Sebulba would be disgraced. The hateful Dug intends to make sure this never happens.

Sebulba is an arboreal Dug from Malastare. Swinging from tree to tree on this high-gravity planet has made Dugs strong and well coordinated. Most have no desire to leave Malastare—and this is fine with the rest of the galaxy since Dugs are notorious bullies.

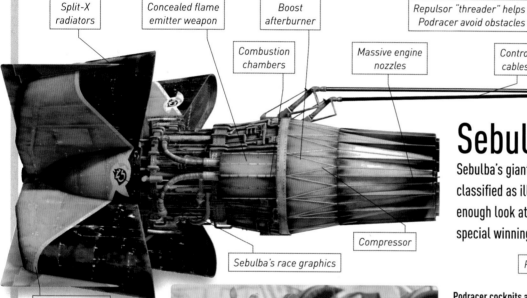

| Split-X radiators | Concealed flame emitter weapon | Boost afterburner | | Repulsor "threader" helps Podracer avoid obstacles |
| Combustion chambers | | Massive engine nozzles | Control cables | |

Control Pod

Sebulba's Podracer

Sebulba's giant Collor Pondrat Plug-F Mammoth Split-X Podracer would be classified as illegally large if race officials were ever able to take a close enough look at it. Concealed weapons like Sebulba's flame emitter lend that special winning edge during a race.

Sebulba's race graphics

Compressor

Stabilizing vane

The race crowds love a winner, and Sebulba delivers victories time and again. The odious Dug plays to the crowd when in their sight, and has become the heavy favorite in the betting pits.

Wattle

Crowd-pleasing grin

Podracer cockpits are customized to suit the particular driver's anatomy. Sebulba's complex array of control pedals and levers is woven into an even more complicated automatic data transmission bank that provides readouts of all engine conditions during the race.

Pre-feed pyrometer readout

Main combustion pyrometer readout

Aeration mix gauge

Second-stage fuel flow rate indicator

Throttle lever

Sebulba, Podrace Anarchist

Sebulba is a highly skilled Podracer, but he was not quite good enough to make it to the top on ability alone. When he found that intimidation and race violations were quite effective in gaining victory, he refined these abilities and began to add secret weapons to his racing machine. Dispatching opponents without getting caught is now the chief sporting aspect of Podracing for the malevolent Dug.

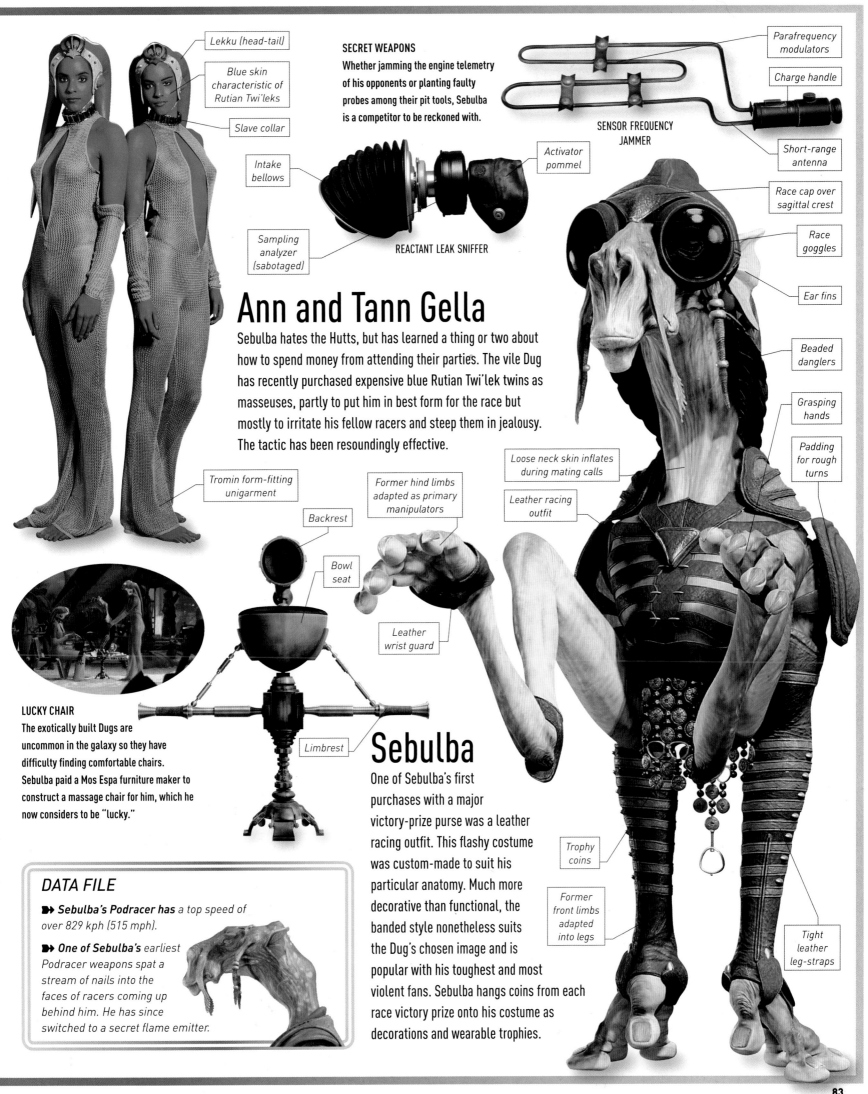

Lekku (head-tail)

Blue skin characteristic of Rutian Twi'leks

Slave collar

SECRET WEAPONS
Whether jamming the engine telemetry of his opponents or planting faulty probes among their pit tools, Sebulba is a competitor to be reckoned with.

Parafrequency modulators

Charge handle

SENSOR FREQUENCY JAMMER

Short-range antenna

Intake bellows

Activator pommel

Sampling analyzer (sabotaged)

REACTANT LEAK SNIFFER

Race cap over sagittal crest

Race goggles

Ear fins

Ann and Tann Gella

Sebulba hates the Hutts, but has learned a thing or two about how to spend money from attending their parties. The vile Dug has recently purchased expensive blue Rutian Twi'lek twins as masseuses, partly to put him in best form for the race but mostly to irritate his fellow racers and steep them in jealousy. The tactic has been resoundingly effective.

Beaded danglers

Grasping hands

Padding for rough turns

Loose neck skin inflates during mating calls

Leather racing outfit

Tromin form-fitting unigarment

Former hind limbs adapted as primary manipulators

Backrest

Bowl seat

Leather wrist guard

LUCKY CHAIR
The exotically built Dugs are uncommon in the galaxy so they have difficulty finding comfortable chairs. Sebulba paid a Mos Espa furniture maker to construct a massage chair for him, which he now considers to be "lucky."

Limbrest

Sebulba

One of Sebulba's first purchases with a major victory-prize purse was a leather racing outfit. This flashy costume was custom-made to suit his particular anatomy. Much more decorative than functional, the banded style nonetheless suits the Dug's chosen image and is popular with his toughest and most violent fans. Sebulba hangs coins from each race victory prize onto his costume as decorations and wearable trophies.

Trophy coins

Former front limbs adapted into legs

Tight leather leg-straps

DATA FILE

➤ **Sebulba's Podracer has** a top speed of over 829 kph (515 mph).

➤ **One of Sebulba's** earliest Podracer weapons spat a stream of nails into the faces of racers coming up behind him. He has since switched to a secret flame emitter.

PODRACER CONTENDERS

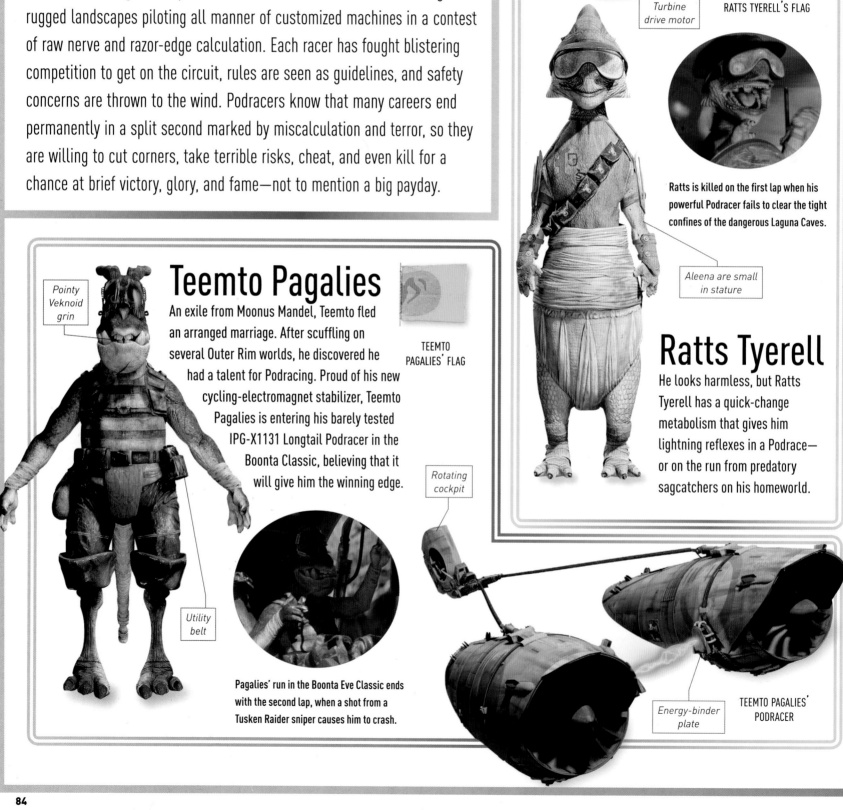

RATTS TYERELL'S PODRACER

Massive intakes

Turbine drive motor

RATTS TYERELL'S FLAG

NOTHING COMPARES TO THE SHEER SPECTACLE of Podracing on the planets of the Outer Rim. Racers tear through rugged landscapes piloting all manner of customized machines in a contest of raw nerve and razor-edge calculation. Each racer has fought blistering competition to get on the circuit, rules are seen as guidelines, and safety concerns are thrown to the wind. Podracers know that many careers end permanently in a split second marked by miscalculation and terror, so they are willing to cut corners, take terrible risks, cheat, and even kill for a chance at brief victory, glory, and fame—not to mention a big payday.

Ratts is killed on the first lap when his powerful Podracer fails to clear the tight confines of the dangerous Laguna Caves.

Aleena are small in stature

Teemto Pagalies

Pointy Veknoid grin

An exile from Moonus Mandel, Teemto fled an arranged marriage. After scuffling on several Outer Rim worlds, he discovered he had a talent for Podracing. Proud of his new cycling-electromagnet stabilizer, Teemto Pagalies is entering his barely tested IPG-X1131 Longtail Podracer in the Boonta Classic, believing that it will give him the winning edge.

TEEMTO PAGALIES' FLAG

Ratts Tyerell

He looks harmless, but Ratts Tyerell has a quick-change metabolism that gives him lightning reflexes in a Podrace— or on the run from predatory sagcatchers on his homeworld.

Rotating cockpit

Utility belt

Pagalies' run in the Boonta Eve Classic ends with the second lap, when a shot from a Tusken Raider sniper causes him to crash.

Energy-binder plate

TEEMTO PAGALIES' PODRACER

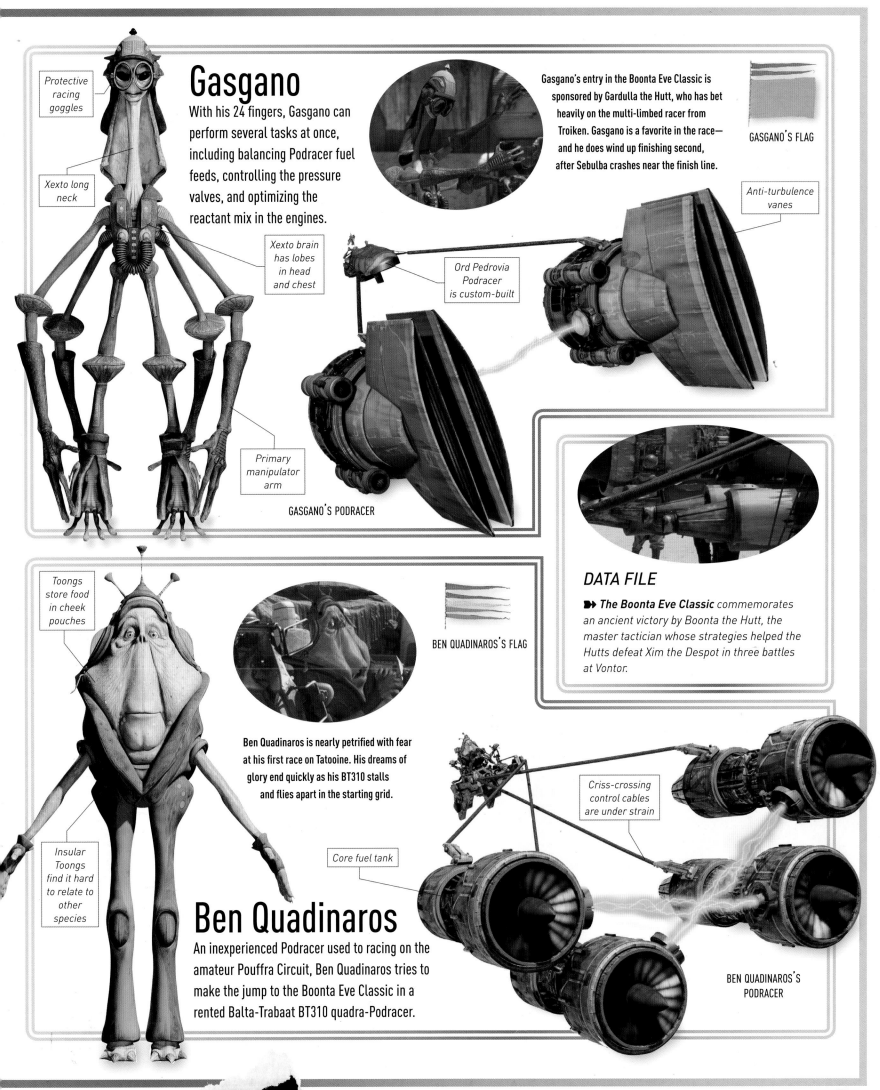

Gasgano

With his 24 fingers, Gasgano can perform several tasks at once, including balancing Podracer fuel feeds, controlling the pressure valves, and optimizing the reactant mix in the engines.

Protective racing goggles

Xexto long neck

Xexto brain has lobes in head and chest

Ord Pedrovia Podracer is custom-built

Primary manipulator arm

GASGANO'S PODRACER

Gasgano's entry in the Boonta Eve Classic is sponsored by Gardulla the Hutt, who has bet heavily on the multi-limbed racer from Troiken. Gasgano is a favorite in the race—and he does wind up finishing second, after Sebulba crashes near the finish line.

GASGANO'S FLAG

Anti-turbulence vanes

DATA FILE

▶ **The Boonta Eve Classic** commemorates an ancient victory by Boonta the Hutt, the master tactician whose strategies helped the Hutts defeat Xim the Despot in three battles at Vontor.

BEN QUADINAROS'S FLAG

Ben Quadinaros is nearly petrified with fear at his first race on Tatooine. His dreams of glory end quickly as his BT310 stalls and flies apart in the starting grid.

Toongs store food in cheek pouches

Insular Toongs find it hard to relate to other species

Criss-crossing control cables are under strain

Core fuel tank

Ben Quadinaros

An inexperienced Podracer used to racing on the amateur Pouffra Circuit, Ben Quadinaros tries to make the jump to the Boonta Eve Classic in a rented Balta-Trabaat BT310 quadra-Podracer.

BEN QUADINAROS'S PODRACER

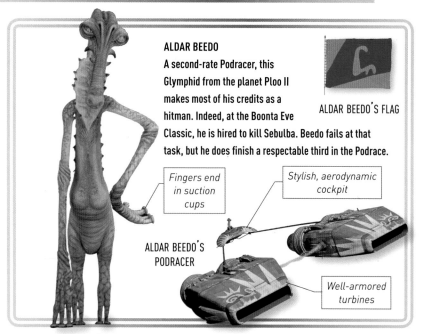

ALDAR BEEDO

A second-rate Podracer, this Glymphid from the planet Ploo II makes most of his credits as a hitman. Indeed, at the Boonta Eve Classic, he is hired to kill Sebulba. Beedo fails at that task, but he does finish a respectable third in the Podrace.

ALDAR BEEDO'S FLAG

Fingers end in suction cups

Stylish, aerodynamic cockpit

ALDAR BEEDO'S PODRACER

Well-armored turbines

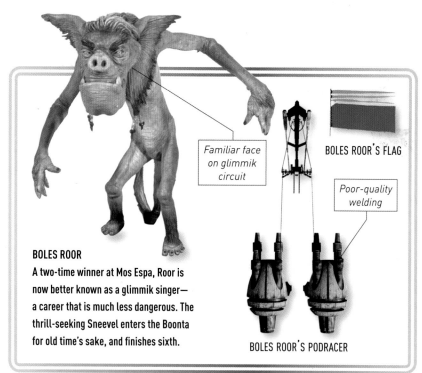

Familiar face on glimmik circuit

BOLES ROOR'S FLAG

Poor-quality welding

BOLES ROOR

A two-time winner at Mos Espa, Roor is now better known as a glimmik singer—a career that is much less dangerous. The thrill-seeking Sneevel enters the Boonta for old time's sake, and finishes sixth.

BOLES ROOR'S PODRACER

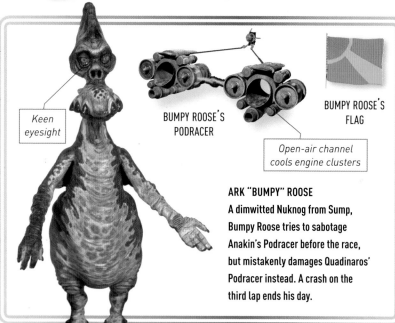

Keen eyesight

BUMPY ROOSE'S PODRACER

BUMPY ROOSE'S FLAG

Open-air channel cools engine clusters

ARK "BUMPY" ROOSE

A dimwitted Nuknog from Sump, Bumpy Roose tries to sabotage Anakin's Podracer before the race, but mistakenly damages Quadinaros' Podracer instead. A crash on the third lap ends his day.

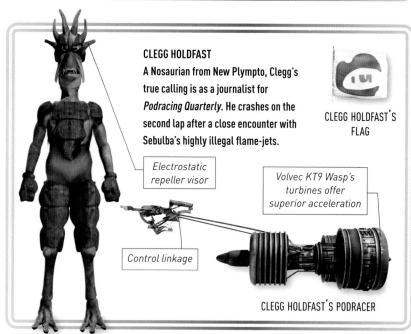

CLEGG HOLDFAST

A Nosaurian from New Plympto, Clegg's true calling is as a journalist for *Podracing Quarterly*. He crashes on the second lap after a close encounter with Sebulba's highly illegal flame-jets.

CLEGG HOLDFAST'S FLAG

Electrostatic repeller visor

Volvec KT9 Wasp's turbines offer superior acceleration

Control linkage

CLEGG HOLDFAST'S PODRACER

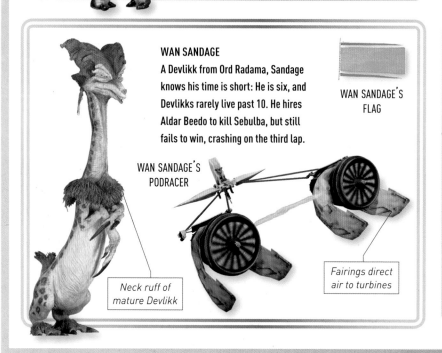

WAN SANDAGE

A Devlikk from Ord Radama, Sandage knows his time is short: He is six, and Devlikks rarely live past 10. He hires Aldar Beedo to kill Sebulba, but still fails to win, crashing on the third lap.

WAN SANDAGE'S FLAG

WAN SANDAGE'S PODRACER

Neck ruff of mature Devlikk

Fairings direct air to turbines

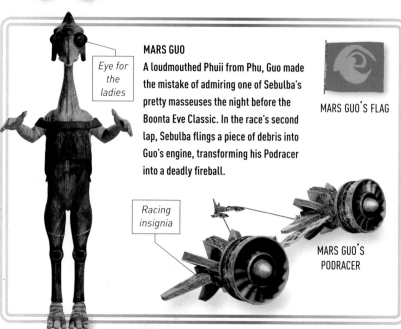

Eye for the ladies

MARS GUO

A loudmouthed Phuii from Phu, Guo made the mistake of admiring one of Sebulba's pretty masseuses the night before the Boonta Eve Classic. In the race's second lap, Sebulba flings a piece of debris into Guo's engine, transforming his Podracer into a deadly fireball.

MARS GUO'S FLAG

Racing insignia

MARS GUO'S PODRACER

NEVA KEE

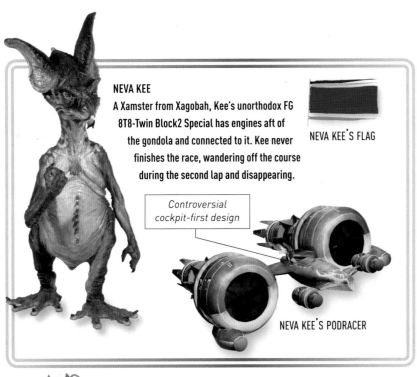

A Xamster from Xagobah, Kee's unorthodox FG 8T8-Twin Block2 Special has engines aft of the gondola and connected to it. Kee never finishes the race, wandering off the course during the second lap and disappearing.

NEVA KEE'S FLAG

Controversial cockpit-first design

NEVA KEE'S PODRACER

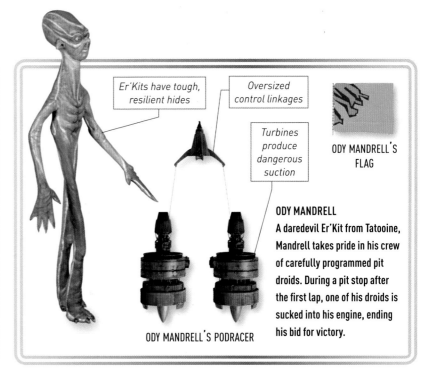

Er'Kits have tough, resilient hides

Oversized control linkages

Turbines produce dangerous suction

ODY MANDRELL'S FLAG

ODY MANDRELL

A daredevil Er'Kit from Tatooine, Mandrell takes pride in his crew of carefully programmed pit droids. During a pit stop after the first lap, one of his droids is sucked into his engine, ending his bid for victory.

ODY MANDRELL'S PODRACER

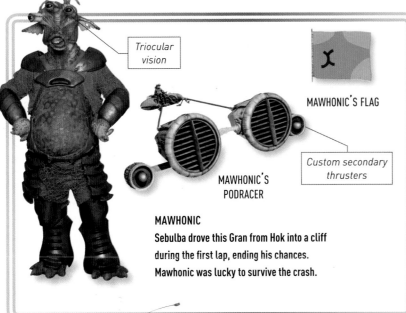

Triocular vision

MAWHONIC'S FLAG

Custom secondary thrusters

MAWHONIC'S PODRACER

MAWHONIC

Sebulba drove this Gran from Hok into a cliff during the first lap, ending his chances. Mawhonic was lucky to survive the crash.

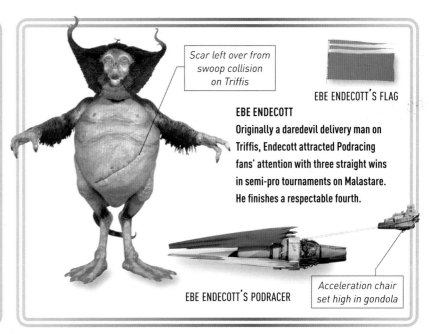

Scar left over from swoop collision on Triffis

EBE ENDECOTT'S FLAG

EBE ENDECOTT

Originally a daredevil delivery man on Triffis, Endecott attracted Podracing fans' attention with three straight wins in semi-pro tournaments on Malastare. He finishes a respectable fourth.

EBE ENDECOTT'S PODRACER

Acceleration chair set high in gondola

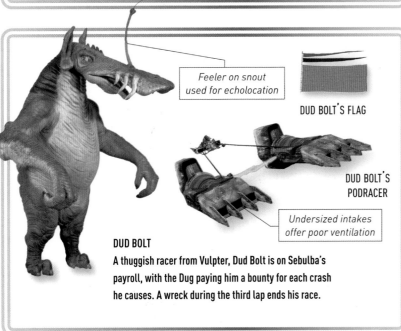

Feeler on snout used for echolocation

DUD BOLT'S FLAG

DUD BOLT'S PODRACER

Undersized intakes offer poor ventilation

DUD BOLT

A thuggish racer from Vulpter, Dud Bolt is on Sebulba's payroll, with the Dug paying him a bounty for each crash he causes. A wreck during the third lap ends his race.

ELAN MAK

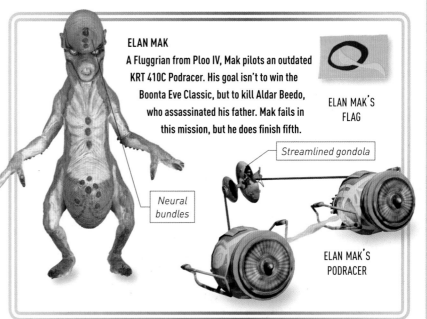

A Fluggrian from Ploo IV, Mak pilots an outdated KRT 410C Podracer. His goal isn't to win the Boonta Eve Classic, but to kill Aldar Beedo, who assassinated his father. Mak fails in this mission, but he does finish fifth.

ELAN MAK'S FLAG

Streamlined gondola

Neural bundles

ELAN MAK'S PODRACER

PODRACE CREWS

PODRACERS ARE COMPLEX MACHINES THAT REQUIRE EXTENSIVE
maintenance and frequent repair. The mechanical stress of running high-performance engines
at up to 800 kilometers per hour takes a heavy toll on any Tatooine Podracer. The pit crews rebuild
the battered machines and prepare them for the next big race. Assisted by frantic pit droids and
pestered by race officials citing violations, Podracer crews must also put up with the egos of the
racers themselves. In spite of it all, the crews take great satisfaction in knowing that they make
all the action possible.

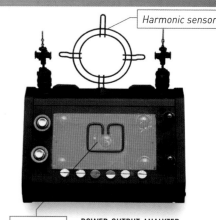

Harmonic sensor

Alignment screen

POWER OUTPUT ANALYZER

Podracing crews use specialized instruments to
analyze engine performance and diagnose faults.
Tools should be standardized for safety and
fairness, but in practice no two crews have the
same gear.

Skylights muted with cloth

Overhead crane track

Massive Podracer engines

Lubricant hoses provide many kinds of oil

Reactant pressurizers

Pit droid

Power cell chargers

Rectifier scale

INSTRUMENT CALIBRATOR

Output sampler

Pit Hangar

In the huge Podracer hangar at Mos Espa Grand
Arena, Podracers are tuned to their best by
busy pit crews until the last minute before a race.
Heavy-duty overhead cranes help with
maintenance and repair. Race officials attempt to
certify the vehicles, but the crews use every tactic
imaginable to distract, threaten, or bribe them.

Heavy cranes move Podracer engines

Sebulba and his slaves on display

Handle

Receiver antenna

IMPULSE DETECTORS
Key parts of every pit mechanic's kit are
impulse detectors, which monitor the
dangerous power outputs of Podracers.
Crews also use detectors to scan rival
racers, signaling their own drivers if they
detect imbalances. Sufficiently dangerous
levels or imbalances would force a racer
to make a pit stop between laps.

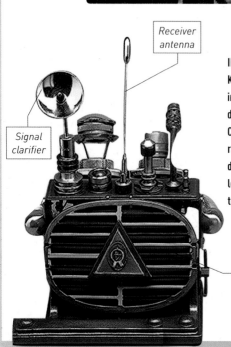

Signal clarifier

Impulse detector unit

Low-frequency enhancer

Impulse probe tip

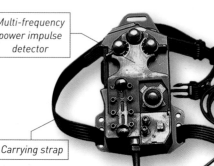

Multi-frequency power impulse detector

Carrying strap

Insulating sleeve

Firing terminal

PODRACER POWER PLUG
Podracers use enormous amounts of energy, and the stresses of racing sometimes rupture power lines, cause systems to overload, or lead to power dips in components. Power plugs are temporary solutions for coaxing a balky racer to the finish line.

Mag-pulse transmitter

COURSE MARKER
Courses are marked by beacons that send pulses to Podracers' navigation systems. Unscrupulous racers sometimes jam course beacons' signals, leaving rivals flying blind.

The mammoth, deafeningly loud turbines of Podracer engines require fine-tuning to make it through a race. The delicate work can often be dangerous, and mechanics must be careful when they are near the engines whether they are ignited or not.

Podrace Mechanics

Humans, who cannot safely pilot the blindingly fast Podracers, often become expert mechanics in Podracer crews. These largely unsung geniuses build some of the best engines for species that can exploit the powerful machines to their fullest capacities.

BOK ASKOL

Polarizing field insulator

Pacithhip mechanic

Utility tool vest

MAT RAGS

Welding goggles

DATA FILE
➼ **Good mechanics are** hard to find, and wise racers pay them well, or risk losing them to a rival's service.

LANA DOBREED

ODIN NESLOOR

PIT DROIDS

PROGRAMMED TO HAVE A PERMANENT SENSE OF urgency, pit droids are utility mechanics that assist with simple maintenance jobs. Their compact form allows them to reach small parts and linkages in and under Podracer engines. Pit droids are built with minimal logic processors so they take orders without asking personal or superfluous questions. However, this also leaves them easily confused and apt to get into trouble when left to their own devices. Their limitations are obvious, but galactic civilization has no shortage of mundane tasks for these diminutive droids. Mechanics soon find themselves grateful for pit droids' assistance and even charmed by their single-minded dedication to their simple duties.

Pit droids are such a common sight near Podracers that they go mostly unnoticed, in spite of the bizarre antics they sometimes engage in when trying to get a job done. The real mechanics are left to make the complex decisions and oversee customized engine modifications.

Droid intercommunication antenna

Head plate protects against falling tools

High-output power source needs frequent recharging

Monocular photoreceptor

Smooth universal joint

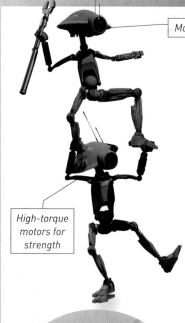

Circus Act

Pit droids are very durable and able to shake off encounters with nearly anything short of a blast furnace. Being more or less invulnerable isn't always a good thing, however: If asked to work on a system they can't reach, pit droids may form swaying mechanical pyramids, hurl each other through the air, or come up with other amazingly bad ideas instead of asking for help.

High-torque motors for strength

Pit droids are so focused on their assigned tasks that they often fail to take other data into account, sometimes with disastrous results. One of Ody Mandrell's pit droids is sucked into the powerful intake of his Podracer's turbine. The pit droid is fine, but Ody's engine is not.

Hardened alloy casing

Tough construction

DATA FILE

➤ **Pit droids were** originally built by Serv-O-Droid for companies on the industrial world of Cyrillia.

➤ **A tap on** the "nose" of a pit droid causes it to collapse into a compressed form for easy storage (and to keep it out of trouble).

Droidwork

Pit droids' simple graspers are built for strength, not precision: Assigning them delicate tasks or giving them complex tools is a recipe for disaster. They're best at simple jobs such as bashing out dents, opening or closing valves, attaching or detaching hoses, or lugging things from one place to another.

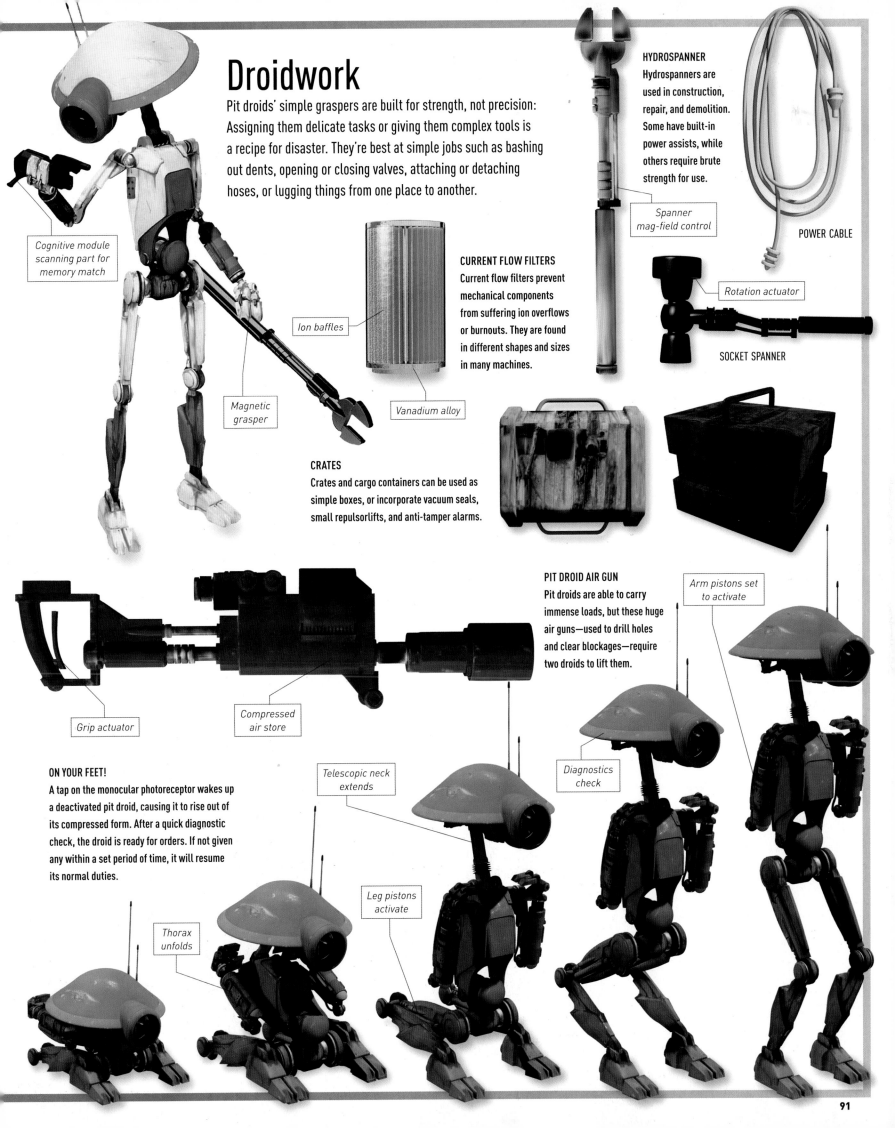

Cognitive module scanning part for memory match

Magnetic grasper

Ion baffles

Vanadium alloy

CURRENT FLOW FILTERS
Current flow filters prevent mechanical components from suffering ion overflows or burnouts. They are found in different shapes and sizes in many machines.

HYDROSPANNER
Hydrospanners are used in construction, repair, and demolition. Some have built-in power assists, while others require brute strength for use.

Spanner mag-field control

POWER CABLE

Rotation actuator

SOCKET SPANNER

CRATES
Crates and cargo containers can be used as simple boxes, or incorporate vacuum seals, small repulsorlifts, and anti-tamper alarms.

Grip actuator

Compressed air store

PIT DROID AIR GUN
Pit droids are able to carry immense loads, but these huge air guns—used to drill holes and clear blockages—require two droids to lift them.

Arm pistons set to activate

Diagnostics check

ON YOUR FEET!
A tap on the monocular photoreceptor wakes up a deactivated pit droid, causing it to rise out of its compressed form. After a quick diagnostic check, the droid is ready for orders. If not given any within a set period of time, it will resume its normal duties.

Telescopic neck extends

Leg pistons activate

Thorax unfolds

THE PODRACE CROWD

FLOONORP   SABRIQUET   DRIXFAR

MOS ESPA ARENA IS BUILT WITHIN A NATURAL CANYON amphitheater on the edge of Tatooine's western Dune Sea. The Boonta Eve Classic is the arena and the planet's premier event, attracting Hutts from the major clans, Podracing enthusiasts, curious tourists, and thousands of Tatooine locals. Box seats are reserved for the wealthy and powerful, while regulars shove their way into the packed, barely policed stands. Gambling is rampant, with bets taken in the arena's halls or by eager touts in the stands.

Mos Espa Arena

The atmosphere before a Podrace is electric. Spectators take their seats in the stands; the rich enter their boxes or elevating platforms for an aerial view; Podracers are prepared in the pit building and the betting floors are scenes of feverish activity as the odds are updated every few seconds.

Premium-priced seats beneath canopies

Concessions concourse

Arena citadel with betting floors

Balloons carry spectators or illegal omnicams

West stands

Viewing platform

Race officials' building

Starters' box

Racers on starting grid

Press building

FANATICAL SPECTATORS
Thousands of race fans fill the vast capacity of Mos Espa Grand Arena for the big races such as the Boonta Eve. Every language in the galaxy is heard from the Podrace enthusiasts as entire fortunes are wagered on current favorites and hopeless longshots.

The starters' box holds race officials, the starting light, and three lap indicators.

The system for determining the starting lineup of the Boonta Eve race involves an apparently baffling combination of performance statistics, outright bribery, and random chance.

Cam Droids

Race cameras used to be built into the rocks along the course to help spectators catch every thrill, but these were all stolen or shot to pieces. Now, a fleet of hovering cam droids is used.

Metal pitted by kicked-up grit

Transmission antenna

Mini-reactor power feeds

SIDE VIEW

Housing set on gyroscopic gimbals

Repulsorlift wing

Each Podracer has a dedicated cam droid

Multiple lenses catch a range of angles on key turns and speed flats

DATA FILE

➤ **Mos Espa Arena** holds more than 100,000 Podrace spectators.

➤ **Race contestants** are granted seating for chosen supporters. Anakin's mother and friends watch the race from an elevating platform.

Podrace Balloons

The Hutts charge fans to use viewscreen channels supplied by official repulsorlift race cameras. However, a gray market of cheap channels fed by balloon cameras has sprung up, since only permanent and repulsorlift-powered cameras are controlled. Some brave spectators even watch the race from rented balloons, which are often shot down by drunk and disorderly fans or angry losing betters.

HANDHELD VIEWSCREENS
Giant screens in the sumptuous levels of the Arena Citadel betting floors monitor the views from the race cameras. However, most fans prefer to watch the race in the stands using rented screens or electrobinoculars.

Stereo-view double eyepieces

Display mode select

Channel select

Grip bars

RACE ELECTROBINOCULARS

Motion-tracking scanner

Double ballonets inside envelope for stability

Supporting framework

High tensile-strength cables

Tibanna gas compound keeps balloon afloat

Patches repair damage from being shot down

Spectator gondola

Jawa-built envelope

Cheap channel race omnicam

Fode and Beed

These flamboyant Podracing announcers are actually a single, two-headed Troig. Fode, the red-skinned head, speaks Basic, while Beed, the green-skinned head, offers running commentary in Huttese.

JABBA'S BOX

NUNA

S OMEWHERE IN MOS ESPA THERE IS A LITTLE-KNOWN figure who "offically" rules the city, but the wealthy gangster "First Citizen" Jabba the Hutt is really in control. Jabba oversees his criminal empire from an old B'omarr monastery in Tatooine's Dune Sea. Jabba's palace is a garden of Huttese delights, but few of its attractions can match the lure of betting on Mos Espa's legendary Podraces. When associates who can't resist a good wager come to call, Jabba sends word to prepare his royal box in Mos Espa Arena, which he financed and where he controls the betting odds. The balcony offers a superb view of the race and is reached from a lavish suite of banquet halls, spice dens, and secret chambers.

Sturdy frame of Ayalayli thornwood

HUTT HEIRLOOM
Jabba's gong is one of the Hutt crimelord's favorite conversation pieces. The dealer who sold it to him swore it was used in the Parliament of Moralan before that species' extinction at the Hutts' hands. A spat-out head striking the gong signals the start of the Boonta Eve Classic.

Brightly colored ruff typical of Theelin

DIVA SHALIQUA
A half-breed Theelin, Diva Shaliqua spent her childhood as a slave in the retinue of Ingoda the Hutt before being sold to Jabba as a court singer.

Secret transmitter installed by former owner Marlo the Hutt

R5-X2
Jabba acquired this astromech as payment of a debt after discovering it had been programmed to run gambling simulations. But R5's recommendations have proved worthless, and Jabba suspects he has been tricked.

Oily secretions keep out Tatooine heat

Raw and wriggling Gorgs are Jabba's choice of snack

Huttese glyphs of good fortune

Bib Fortuna, Jabba's Twi'lek major-domo

Jabba's shisha

Diva Shaliqua, one of Jabba's slaves

Diva Funquita, Gardulla's assistant

Gardulla the Hutt, Jabba's guest and sometime rival

Jabba the Hutt

Dwarf nunas brought back by one of Jabba's assassins from a recent mission

Jabba the Hutt

Jabba presides over the Boonta Eve race from the best box seats in the arena, decorated with Hutt clan banners, trophies from ancient Hutt conquests, and conversation pieces from Jabba's collection. His major-domo Bib Fortuna attends to every arrangement, keeping Jabba's entertainment running as smoothly as his criminal operations. At Mos Espa, Jabba revels in the thought of the profits he will reap through his gambling organizations.

Muscular tail can deliver powerful blows

Gardulla the Hutt battles with Jabba for control of Tatooine's black market. A chronic gambler, Gardulla has lost countless assets making bets.

Aurra Sing is surrounded by rumors: it is claimed she is an Anzati vampire, a failed Padawan, a Hutt-built cyborg, or a Clawdite shape-shifter.

CANYON LOOKOUT
As the Podracers race through the tight confines of Beggar's Canyon, Aurra watches from the vantage point of a cliffside hermitage. She doesn't interfere with the race, intent on a mysterious mission known only to her.

Antenna connects to internal biocomputer

Slugthrower fires solid projectiles

BIB FORTUNA
A former spice smuggler and slave trader, Bib Fortuna looks after Jabba's affairs in Tatooine's towns and in his sprawling Dune Sea palace. Jabba takes great pleasure in tormenting the touchy, squeamish Twi'lek major-domo.

Long, skeletal fingers

Sensitive lekku

Well-worn grip

DX-13 modified for dual triggers

Multi-spectrum targeting scope

CUSTOMIZED PISTOLS
Aurra carries two DX-13 pistols customized to feature dual triggers. The front triggers are more comfortable for her unnaturally long fingers, and require more pressure to fire, while the back triggers are rigged for rapid fire.

LONG-RANGE RIFLE
A good sniper needs keen eyesight, steady hands, and uncanny patience, and Aurra possesses all three skills. Once she locates her bounties, Aurra uses her long-barreled Czerka Adventurer rifle to neutralize targets from incredible distances.

Utility pouches

Aurra Sing
The mysterious Aurra Sing is wanted in dozens of systems for crimes committed as an assassin, pirate, and bounty hunter. She works for anyone who has the credits, but harbors a particular hatred of Jedi. Known aliases include Nashtah and Shatta Aunuanna.

Soft-soled shoes

Holsters made of shaak hide

Prized boots of rancor skin

TATOOINE INHABITANTS

A FRONTIER WORLD, THE DESERT PLANET TATOOINE LIES ON AN IMPORTANT HYPERSPACE route between the civilized planets of the galactic core and the lawless star systems of the Outer Rim. Traders and smugglers run all manner of goods through Tatooine's spaceports, answering to few authorities besides the gangster Hutts. On the desert surface, inhabitants include desperate settlers, impoverished spacers, aliens of dubious reputation, droids of all kinds, along with the scattered representatives of Tatooine's native populations, who are best adapted to life on this difficult world.

Teguar deal-maker

Retractable awning

Gorg dipping sauces

Amphibious gorgs cooked at street stalls

Non-indigenous species recovered from freighter bilge

Locals keep a low profile

Jedi Quinlan Vos on secret mission

R2-D2

The slave Erdan was chemically enlarged by his owner to increase his work-rate. His face was patterned as a mark of ownership.

GORGMONGER
Gragra claims to keep her amphibian food stock in a large basement culture pool, but she actually grows them in a sewer zone under Mos Espa.

Not everyone in Mos Espa is a gangster or spacer. Many residents scrape by, dreaming of the day their luck will finally change.

Stranded gambler Yade M'rak

Notorious infochant Televan Koreyy

Marketplace

In the crowded marketplace alleys of Mos Espa, various quarters specialize in particular types of trade. Some serve the day-to-day needs of local inhabitants, while others house droid mechanics, engine repairers, and—if you know where to look—illegal weapons dealers.

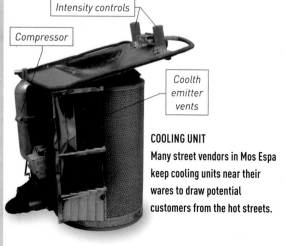

Intensity controls

Compressor

Coolth emitter vents

COOLING UNIT
Many street vendors in Mos Espa keep cooling units near their wares to draw potential customers from the hot streets.

Spacers willing to run routes into the risky areas beyond Tatooine wait for work in a streetside café, where cooled table slabs offer some respite from the heat. Games like triga help to pass the time.

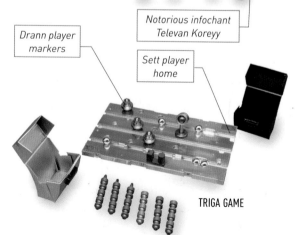

Drann player markers

Sett player home

TRIGA GAME

Handle

SANDSTAT
Sand and dust blows into every corner of Mos Espa; the fastidious clean up with electrostatic sandstats.

Collector

Intake

Ion charger exhaust

Long barrel for accuracy

Gaffi stick

Stolen projectile rifle

Bound hands

Sandproof bindings

Filtering sandmask

Protective eye lenses

Ammo bandoleer

Clan-crafted leatherwork

Sling

Power cell

Heavy cloak and bindings protect against sand and sun

BACKPACK COOLERS
Twin suns make for searing hot middays, so pedestrians in Mos Espa often wear personal cooling units.

Long robe allows free movement and ventilation

At times, Sand People steal guns but strongly favor traditional club and ax weapons for close quarters combat.

Sand People take pot shots at fast-moving Podracers from remote sections of the Podrace course, hoping to strand and attack race pilots.

Sand People

Unlike the Jawas, Tatooine's native Sand People have not adapted to the presence of outworld settlers. Resentful of incursions into their territory, they prey upon travelers and raid settlements, torturing captives under the direction of their tribal shamans. Savage and dangerous, they are not to be trifled with.

JAWAS
Indigenous to Tatooine, Jawas have become used to contact with space travelers. Many Jawas act as metal scavengers and equipment-repair craftworkers.

Bandaged feet

Desert Beasts

Tatooine's heat, dust, and sandstorms can damage mechanical transport, but animals such as dewbacks and eopies make ideal beasts of burden. Dewbacks are used all over Tatooine, but eopies are common only around Mos Espa. When the day's work is over, sketto creatures emerge to create a nighttime hazard for beasts of any size and occupation.

SKETTOS

Skettos are cave-dwelling reptomammals that use their four wings to take to Tatooine's skies from dusk until dawn. Their diet is mostly insects, but they do suck blood from large animals while they sleep. Sketto swarms are rare but dangerous, as with sufficient numbers they can overwhelm and kill even large creatures.

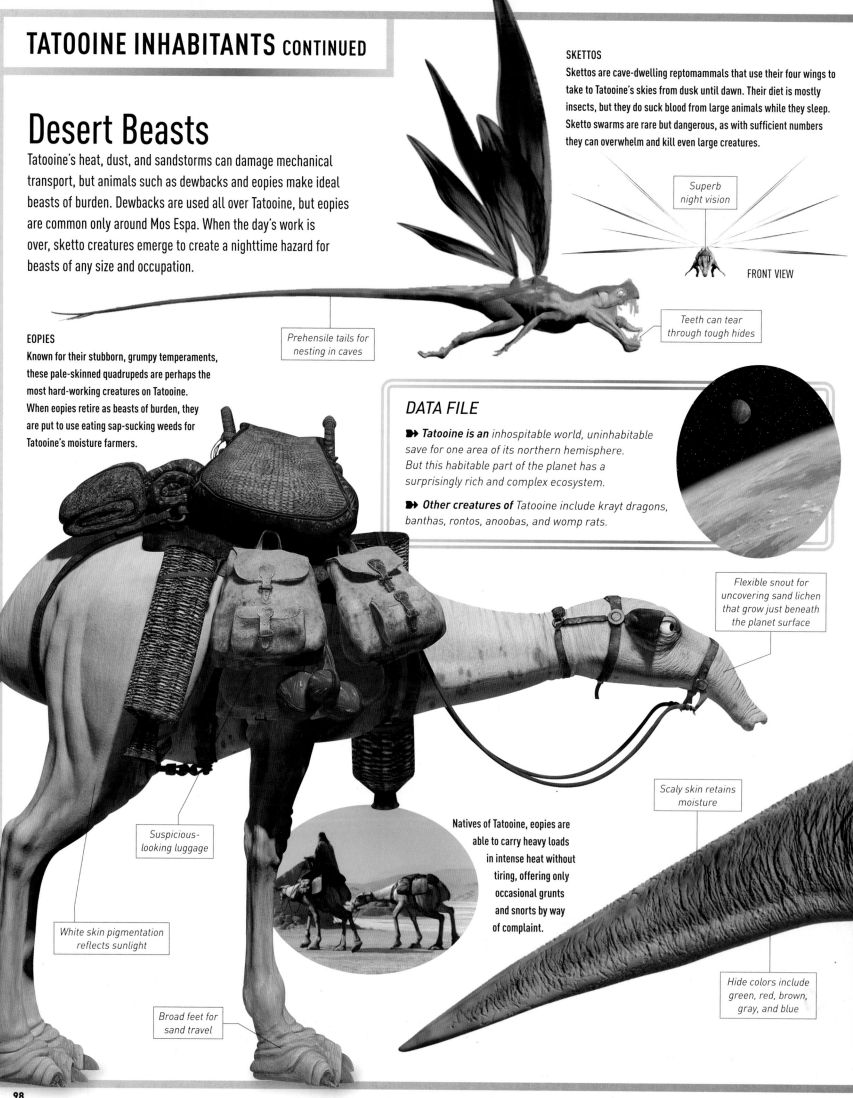

Superb night vision

FRONT VIEW

Teeth can tear through tough hides

Prehensile tails for nesting in caves

EOPIES

Known for their stubborn, grumpy temperaments, these pale-skinned quadrupeds are perhaps the most hard-working creatures on Tatooine. When eopies retire as beasts of burden, they are put to use eating sap-sucking weeds for Tatooine's moisture farmers.

DATA FILE

➤ **Tatooine is an** inhospitable world, uninhabitable save for one area of its northern hemisphere. But this habitable part of the planet has a surprisingly rich and complex ecosystem.

➤ **Other creatures of** Tatooine include krayt dragons, banthas, rontos, anoobas, and womp rats.

Flexible snout for uncovering sand lichen that grow just beneath the planet surface

Suspicious-looking luggage

Natives of Tatooine, eopies are able to carry heavy loads in intense heat without tiring, offering only occasional grunts and snorts by way of complaint.

White skin pigmentation reflects sunlight

Scaly skin retains moisture

Broad feet for sand travel

Hide colors include green, red, brown, gray, and blue

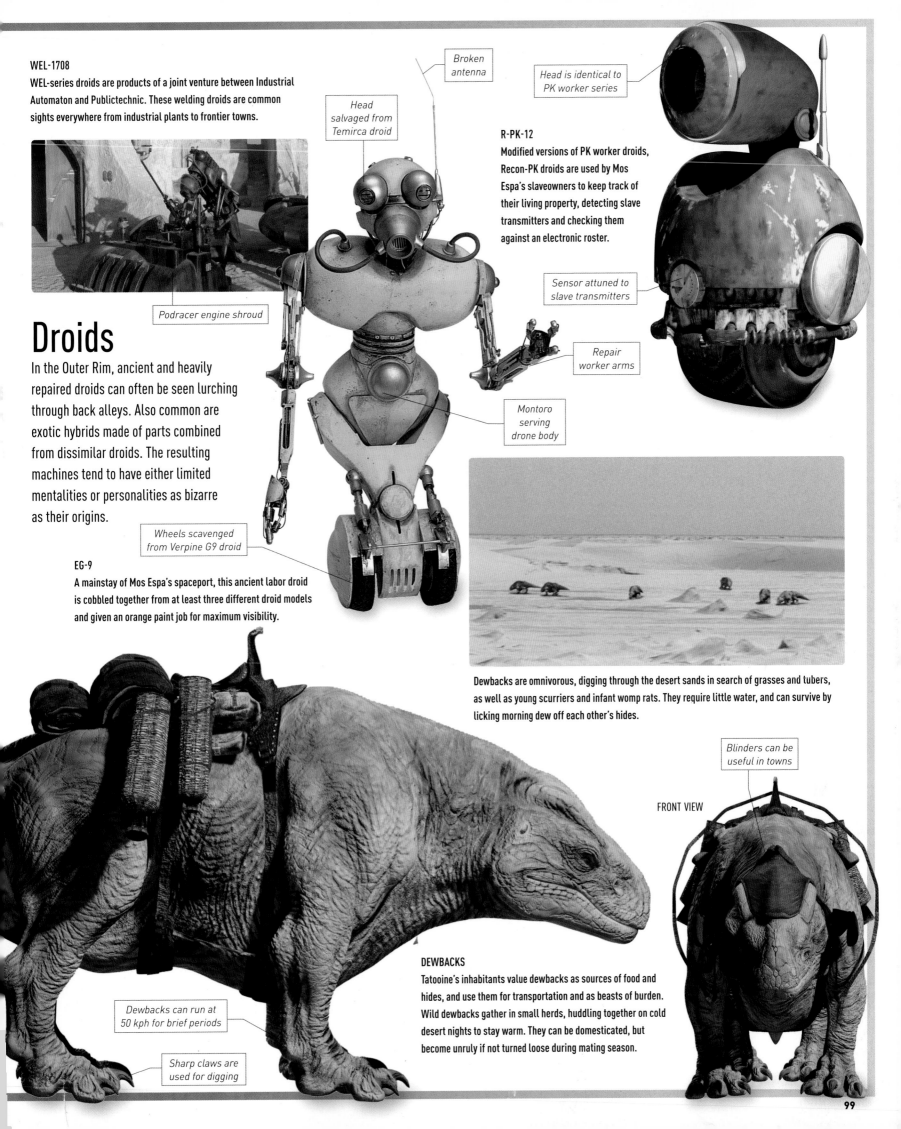

WEL-1708

WEL-series droids are products of a joint venture between Industrial Automaton and Publictechnic. These welding droids are common sights everywhere from industrial plants to frontier towns.

Head salvaged from Temirca droid

Broken antenna

Podracer engine shroud

Droids

In the Outer Rim, ancient and heavily repaired droids can often be seen lurching through back alleys. Also common are exotic hybrids made of parts combined from dissimilar droids. The resulting machines tend to have either limited mentalities or personalities as bizarre as their origins.

Wheels scavenged from Verpine G9 droid

EG-9

A mainstay of Mos Espa's spaceport, this ancient labor droid is cobbled together from at least three different droid models and given an orange paint job for maximum visibility.

Head is identical to PK worker series

R-PK-12

Modified versions of PK worker droids, Recon-PK droids are used by Mos Espa's slaveowners to keep track of their living property, detecting slave transmitters and checking them against an electronic roster.

Sensor attuned to slave transmitters

Repair worker arms

Montoro serving drone body

Dewbacks are omnivorous, digging through the desert sands in search of grasses and tubers, as well as young scurriers and infant womp rats. They require little water, and can survive by licking morning dew off each other's hides.

Blinders can be useful in towns

FRONT VIEW

Dewbacks can run at 50 kph for brief periods

Sharp claws are used for digging

DEWBACKS

Tatooine's inhabitants value dewbacks as sources of food and hides, and use them for transportation and as beasts of burden. Wild dewbacks gather in small herds, huddling together on cold desert nights to stay warm. They can be domesticated, but become unruly if not turned loose during mating season.

THE SENATE

THE POWER OF SECTORIAL SENATORS IS immense, as they control access to the Senate for hundreds of planets. The temptations that go with such power are equally great. Corrupt senators are no longer unusual, even at the highest level, and few Republic citizens expect anything but empty promises and word games from anyone who sets foot on Coruscant. In truth, many senators are lazy and greedy, but by doing nothing to stop the spread of evil they become some of its greatest supporters.

Gesture showing objection

Gesture denying guilt

Gesture blaming others

Gesture of reassurance

MOT-NOT RAB

AKS MOE

PASSEL ARGENTE

HOROX RYYDER

SENATORIAL POLITICS

Many senators have become known for judicious nonalignment, allowing their worlds to profit from supplying both sides in conflicts. Critics comment that three-eyed Malastarians like Baskol Yeesrim can not only see both sides of an issue, but can always spot their position of advantage right in the center.

Consorts

Senators are attended by assistants, aides, and consorts according to customs and traditions of their home planets and sectors. Many young aides are repulsed by the abuses of government they see on Coruscant, but they stay on, reluctant to lose their positions of power.

Rare red-skinned Lethan Twi'lek

Lekku (head-tail)

Ear flaps store fat

Gaudy robe

Senator Orn Free Taa

Indulgent lifestyles are nowhere more extreme than on Coruscant. Senator Orn Free Taa has found possibilities beyond his wildest dreams. He views galactic government as merely the sport of the mighty like himself. In his excesses he has grown vile and corpulent, but he is confident that money and power will always make him attractive.

Senator Tonbuck Toora's last traces of idealism have been eradicated by watching the downfall of the just and from counting the profits that flow from finding loopholes in the law. She now counts as friends criminal senators she once held in contempt and rewards loyal supporters with well-paid appointments as consorts or aides.

CONSORT TO TOONBUCK TOORA

DATA FILE

▶▶ **Lavender was chosen** for the color of the Senate interior because it was the only hue that had never been associated with war, anger, or mourning in any culture in the Republic.

▶▶ **Senator Tikkes moved** from business to Coruscant politics to make some real money.

Senate Guard

The guards of the Galactic Senate wear striking robes of blue, symbolizing the Senate's supreme authority and the long tradition of its wise and just rule. The large crest and simple drape are ceremonial effects rather than functional designs.

When a senate representative is recognized for official speech, their senate platform detaches itself from the Rotunda and flies out into the open chamber for prominence.

Muzzle brake dampens rifle blast

Highly visible crest

ONACONDA FARR

Large, unwieldy ceremonial rifle

Chancellor's podium

Platform housing speaking Senator

SENATE ROTUNDA

The Senate Rotunda contains 1,024 platforms reserved for the galaxy's sectorial Senators, who represent all worlds in their sectors. Senators sometimes lend their platforms to planets or interests with special causes to bring before the Senate. Others have surrendered their right to representation to mercantile powers such as the Trade Federation.

Senate guard

Platform seating

Repulsor lift

SENATE PLATFORMS

Senators undock their platforms from the Rotunda to indicate they wish to speak. After obtaining clearance to address the Senate, they navigate toward the Chancellor's podium, pursued by cam droids.

HOVERCAM SIDE VIEW

Control antenna

Telephoto lens

Wide angle lens

Hovercam

A squadron of flying hovercams patrols the Rotunda to record the speeches and votes of the Senate representatives. Some hovercam operators abuse their responsibility and omit to record certain individuals, while others allow unscrupulous senators to alter the record of their words after they are spoken.

Repulsor floaters

THE DIVERSITY OF THE SENATE

A vast range of alien species populates the Senate Rotunda, hailing from every corner of the Republic. Among them can be seen the traditional costumes of hundreds of planets, as well as many fashions particular to Coruscant.

Dual mouths for stereo language

Brain in neck hump

SENATOR YARUA FROM KASHYYYK

Alderaan aides

Renowned for their tempers, Wookiee senators are nonetheless possessed of a firm sense of fair justice. Senator Yarua finds commercial power within the senate reprehensible and is determined to restore justice to galactic government.

LIANA MERIAN   AGRIPPA ALDRETE   TENDAU BENDON

CHANCELLOR VALORUM

Distinguished gray hair

Premature aging from pressures of governing

Veda cloth robe

A LIFETIME OF PREPARATION LED TO FINIS VALORUM'S ELECTION as Supreme Chancellor of the Galactic Senate. House Valorum has been one of the Republic's most distinguished families for millennia, with several Valorums serving as Supreme Chancellors. Finis Valorum has now equalled this achievement, ruling the entire Republic from the galactic seat on Coruscant. However, he has also inherited a government grown weak from its own success: Galactic representatives have become distanced from their people and the entire system is degenerating.

Helping an Ally

Battling whispers of corruption and debates about taxation, Valorum seeks to help his ally Palpatine by ending the Naboo crisis. He secretly sends Jedi Knights to force the Trade Federation to lift its blockade.

Guard station

SENATE SHUTTLE Valorum and Senators travel around Coruscant in *Eddicus*-class planetary shuttles, equipped with powerful deflector shields to ensure their safety. Senator Palpatine helped guide the *Eddicus* contract to Kuat Systems Engineering.

Blue band symbolic of Supreme Chancellor

DATA FILE

➡ **Coruscant has been** the center of galactic government for tens of thousands of years. Its early history is shrouded in legend.

➡ **Increasingly, Supreme Chancellor** Valorum has been influenced by senators such as Palpatine to compromise what he knows is right for the sake of approved procedure.

Septsilk robe signifies wealth

Ornate overcloak

Sei Taria

Chancellor Valorum's administrative aide, Sei Taria assists him in confirming the fine details of necessary procedural regulations. She has learned much from Senator Palpatine.

Chagrian horns used for intimidating display

Blue skin screens out harmful radiation

Lethorns

Mas Amedda

The stern Chagrian Mas Amedda is responsible for keeping order in the Senate. Accused of misusing his parliamentary powers for bribes, Amedda stands firm to his own code of honor.

SENATOR PALPATINE

ENDLESS PATIENCE HAS BEEN PALPATINE'S KEY TO SUCCESS.
Passed over as a young politician and repeatedly turned down for offices and appointments, he has learned the value of quiet persistence. Palpatine has risen through the ranks to become the Chommell sector's senator on Coruscant, and represents 36 major worlds in his backwater sector, most notably his home planet of Naboo. Turning this background to his advantage, Palpatine has been ever-present in the halls of galactic politics, impressing friend and foe alike with his unassuming demeanor and simple but powerful ideas about how the galaxy could be better run.

Diplomat

Palpatine never favored Naboo's previous sovereign, King Veruna, even after the stubborn ruler heeded Palpatine's suggestions to become more involved in foreign affairs. Queen Amidala suits Palpatine, since he believes she will better follow his directions.

Blue color hints at Palpatine's interest in the Chancellorship

Naboo-style bloused sleeves with long cuffs

Before they meet at the Senate, Queen Amidala has only seen Palpatine in person once, at her coronation. She half-suspects that his concern for Naboo is secondary to his political ambitions.

Elaborate cloak asserts authority

STAR SHUTTLE *PERPETUUS*
Elected chancellor, Palpatine returns to Naboo in a Star Shuttle, commonly used for official travel.

Royal handmaiden

Palpatine's apartment is modest compared to the stunning palaces of other sectorial representatives

Strange red decor

Queen Amidala

PALPATINE'S APARTMENT
Few outsiders are welcomed into Palpatine's scarlet chambers. They are the exclusive haunt of his trusted confidants until Amidala arrives on Coruscant to plead her case.

Over time Palpatine has developed a reputation as someone apart from intrigue and corruption, as he patiently condemns the many abuses of bureaucracy that come to his attention. It is little surprise to insiders that he is nominated for the office of Supreme Chancellor.

DATA FILE

➺ **Senator Palpatine's unusual** choice of art objects reveals to Queen Amidala that he has left his Naboo heritage far behind and has adopted a more worldly point of view.

ROUTE TO SUCCESS
Palpatine consistently favors less concern for senatorial legality and procedure and more attention to simply doing what he considers needs to be done. It is as a result of this practical attitude that many look forward to the clear-minded leadership that Palpatine promises to provide.

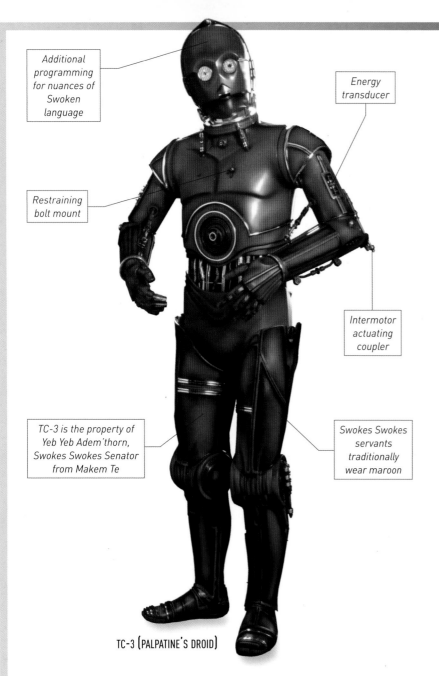

Additional programming for nuances of Swoken language

Energy transducer

Restraining bolt mount

Intermotor actuating coupler

TC-3 is the property of Yeb Yeb Adem'thorn, Swokes Swokes Senator from Makem Te

Swokes Swokes servants traditionally wear maroon

TC-3 (PALPATINE'S DROID)

ACKNOWLEDGMENTS

Jason Fry would like to thank all the talented authors and artists who built upon the story and vision of Episode I with new stories, settings, characters, and lore. Their efforts provided him with countless hours of entertainment as a reader and made updating this Visual Dictionary much easier as a writer.

Dorling Kindersley would like to thank Jo Casey, Emma Grange, Julia March, and Lisa Stock for their editorial work.

Special thanks to modelmaker Neil Ellis for his work on the Darth Maul lightsaber cross-section; Chris Trevas for letting us peek inside the Jedi food and energy capsules with his model; Ed Maggiani and Steve Dymszo for Yoda's custom-made lightsaber; and ILM modelmaker Don Bies, who cracked open the battle droid head for the original book.

Thanks also to Hasbro for allowing the use of their Darth Maul lightsaber toy as the shell for the cross-section model, and to Staedtler for the liquid point pen caps that form part of the Jedi food and energy capsules.

LONDON, NEW YORK, MUNICH, MELBOURNE, AND DELHI

EDITOR HANNAH DOLAN
SENIOR DESIGNER LISA SODEAU
ADDITIONAL DESIGN OWEN BENNETT, LYNNE MOULDING, AND RHYS THOMAS
MANAGING ART EDITOR RON STOBBART
PUBLISHING MANAGER CATHERINE SAUNDERS
ART DIRECTOR LISA LANZARINI
PUBLISHER SIMON BEECROFT
PUBLISHING DIRECTOR ALEX ALLAN
SENIOR PRODUCTION EDITOR JENNIFER MURRAY
PRODUCTION CONTROLLERS MAN FAI LAU AND NICK SESTON

AT LUCASFILM
EXECUTIVE EDITOR J. W. RINZLER
KEEPER OF THE HOLOCRON LELAND CHEE
IMAGE ARCHIVES TINA MILLS, MATTHEW AZEVEDA, AND STACEY LONG
ART DIRECTOR TROY ALDERS
DIRECTOR OF PUBLISHING CAROL ROEDER

First published in the United States in 1999 by DK Publishing, 375 Hudson Street, New York, New York 10014. Revised edition published 2012.

10 9 8 7 6 5 4 3 2 1
001-182976-Jan/12

Page design copyright ©2012 Dorling Kindersley Limited.

A CIP catalog record for this book is available from the Library of Congress.

ISBN 978-0-7566-8995-7

Color reproduction by Scanhouse UK Limited
Printed and bound in China by Leo Paper Products Limited

Discover more at
WWW.DK.COM

Visit the official *Star Wars* site:
WWW.STARWARS.COM